A Woman's Guide to running

'An incredibly practical, down to earth, yet highly motivating guide to running. The book is enlightening and stimulating, illustrating running as a means of achieving other goals and adding value to one's purpose in life. I believe it has a potentially wide appeal to any women in sport...after all, running forms the basis of most physical conditioning programmes in almost all sports.'

Allison Roe (Former Marathon World Champion)

'Today there are millions of women running for health and fitness as well as for competitions. Annemarie Jutel provides expert advice gained through 23 years of running. I believe this is a book women runners should read so as to understand how to achieve improved results both competitively and health-wise and avoid injuries and setbacks.'

Arthur Lydiard (Internationally-acclaimed Running Coach)

'All of us want to get better in our running, we want to enjoy it forever, and know how our body works. Who better to tell us than Annemarie Jutel, a running nurse who's trained herself through kids and late-night jobs and is still improving? Most of us could never be Olympic champions, but Annemarie is like us and with this practical and fun-to-read guide, tells us how we can be the champions inside ourselves.'

Kathrine Switzer (Pioneering Woman Marathoner)

Annemarie Jutel has been running competitively for 30 years. She is a pioneer in women's distance running, a registered nurse with a PhD in physical education, and a prolific writer on sport and running. She lives in New Zealand with her husband and two children and she lectures and researches at the University of Otago.

A
Woman's Guide
to
Running

Beginner to Elite

ANNEMARIE JUTEL

Published in Great Britain by The Women's Press Ltd, 2001
A member of the Namara Group
34 Great Sutton Street,
London EC1V 0LQ
www.the-womens-press.com

First published in New Zealand by Longacre Press Ltd, 1995

British Library Cataloguing-in-Publication Data
A catalogue record for this book is available from the British Library.

ISBN 0 7043 4722 9

The following photographs are reproduced courtesy of:
Jonathan Cameron 139; Juan Colón 98; Reg Graham 26, 120; V. Jacques 19; Thierry Jutel 8, 43, 132.

Typeset in FiSH Books, London WC1
Printed and bound in Great Britain by CPD (Wales) Ltd, Ebbw Vale

To the memory of Christian Bardon,
who taught me, and so many others,
about my own role in fitness
and performance.

'Etre athlète, c'est être responsable'

ACKNOWLEDGEMENTS

I would like to thank the many people who helped me in the realisation of this book, most particularly:

Philippe Alliot, Claude Boumard, Charlotte Cox, John Dolan, Laurence Foucault-Guérineau, Phil Handcock, Glenys Henshaw, Longacre Press, Arthur Lydiard, Lorraine Moller, Reebok (NZ) Ltd, Allison Roe, Sarah Rees, Erin Andersen, Kari Sleivert and Kathrine Switzer.

Also to all those friends in running (and in life!) who have egged me on, cajoled me, persecuted me, supported me, tolerated me and run with me:

My husband, Thierry Jutel, my children, Olivier and Mélanie, François and Marie Guinard, Laurence Parmentier, Douglas Van Zoeren, William Witten, Joel Menges, Doug Horn, John Davis, Willie Griffin, John Connelly, Mr. Engle and Mr. Wilson, Gord Sleivert, Robin Day, John Campbell, Andrews Peskett and Reid, Jeni Dowall, and all the others.

Contents

Introduction

Fitness seems to be constantly in the spotlight these days. Adorable young women are bouncing up and down the footpaths all over town! The hot pink leotards and flashy tights of aerobics confront our eyes at every turn. It doesn't always seem like the real world, however. A lot of us wish we had the time and the body to carry on in that manner, but between full-time work, a houseful of kids, career plans, and several extra pounds, it is hard to believe that this is for everyone. We are not all silly enough to believe the fitness industry's claims: '*Wear our shoes and climb to the stars!*' '*You'll look sleek and sexy in these Lycra tights – the brighter the better!*' All it takes is putting on the shoes, and running around the block to bring us back to reality. It is intimidating and frustrating.

There is something different about running. It is not a new sport which has been created by a fitness industry. Running is not just a fad. Running is the first game you ever played, because as soon as you took your first tottering steps, you were intrigued, and tried to go faster and faster. Pretty soon, you ran everywhere! It was much more exciting than walking. Running belongs to you. Your pace depends on yourself, and not on your team-mates. You are free of all restraints: free to trot, or to gallop.

Running does not require huge amounts of time. All you need are your two legs, and a pair of shoes. To run, you just walk out of the front door, and there you are on the playing field! No need for equipment of any kind! You don't need to go to a court, or a gym to run. You don't need to spend money on a club membership, on rackets or wheels. You don't need to wait for a friend to be free at the same time as you, because you can run alone, as well as with friends. For a busy woman, running is the most efficient way of obtaining complete exercise with minimal time. You can run as much as you want: 15 minutes three times a week, or an hour or more every day. It is up to you to choose the routine which suits your lifestyle.

Running is an efficient sport which provides you with excellent cardiac and neuro-muscular conditioning with minimal investment. With only one hour, spread over the week, you can make tremendous gains.

For a previously inactive woman, running is an excellent initiation to fitness and well-being. Running is the base for almost all other sports, and it has the flexibility that a mother, a career woman, or anyone else with a busy lifestyle needs.

I have been running since the age of thirteen. I chose running as my sport almost by accident, and without being strongly motivated at the start. Twenty-three years and many thousands of miles later, I am grateful for what running has brought me, and the positive ways in which it has changed my life. Of course, I am a competitive runner, and my personal investment in running is immense. My weekends are often devoted to races, and my evenings to running. I am happy to be in a world of men and women who are fit and happy in their bodies. I also savour the time I spend running, when I am alone with my legs, on a shaded track or a city footpath. I spend time with myself, I think, plan, dream. My thighs are strong, my tummy is flat, and I feel good in my body and in my mind.

The busy lifestyle of a woman can be far more demanding than that of a man, especially if she is raising children. I have two children and I work full-time as a nurse and a writer, and I know that my running helps me to survive, keeps me sane, nurtures my patience, and my ability to cope. As a fit woman I can face the world on my own two feet. As a nurse, I am constantly aware of just how important fitness can be in the prevention of illness, and how serious the consequences of inactivity can be on the body, mind and soul.

We can all run! It doesn't need to be puff and grunt, sweat and tears. It is a gentle sport that doesn't need to hurt. Toss the 'no pain, no gain!' philosophy out the door, and come for a run!

IS RUNNING FOR YOU?

If you have gone so far as to pick up this book, and read up to this page, there must be a tiny spark of interest somewhere. If that is the case, then the answer to the above question is an overwhelming, enthusiastic and definite 'yes!' Again, thinking back to basics, you never asked if running was for you when you started your pedestrian approach to life at age one or two. You just assumed that running was the way to get places. Many of us were conditioned not to run by going to school where we sat still for many hours a day, or by parents, who were less in a hurry than we were. 'Annemarie! Come back here!' or 'wait for the rest of us!' Growing up seems to have an unfortunate settling effect. Remember, our bodies were made to run – we just have to get beyond the rules and regulations, and the artificial barriers that have taken the run and skip out of our lives. If you can identify yourself in any of the categories described below, then, yes, running has something to offer you. Read on.

You like to spend a few minutes away from the fast track

What better way to get out of the rat race than to put on a pair of running shoes, and blow off some steam! Running can help you to cope with the stress of work and family life, by providing you with a readily available physical outlet. It gives you a little time to be on your own, and to think things through. It allows you to maintain a bit of space and quiet in your otherwise busy existence.

You want your body to be trimmer than it is right now

Running is a complete sport which can help you to regain both fitness and self-esteem. What's more, it is not as intimidating as some activities that take place in enclosed settings like a gym or a pool where you feel like everyone might be looking at you, or where you might be constantly measuring yourself up against every person in town.

You feel good about your body and want to give running a try

Running is a continuous review and discovery of your physical limits. The exploration is fascinating, and each stride takes you further in that personal exploration.

There are many barriers we tend to put

When 34 year old Priscilla Welch first started running in 1978, she was unemployed and simply looking to get a bit fitter. She entered her first race, despite misgivings, after encouragement from her husband. She thought that she was too old for competitive running. After blazing through the 10 kilometre cross-country race in 42 minutes, onlookers were quickly convinced that here was a fit and talented runner.

The follow up to this story is well known to the international road-running community today. Priscilla Welch went on to be the best female veteran distance runner in the world. Her accomplishments include a 32:15 10 kms, a 1h 11 half marathon, and a 2h 26 marathon, while well into her 40s. She is an international leader, stronger than runners half her age.

up in our minds against starting a running programme, and these need to be addressed. You may recognise some of the following.

You feel low on energy, and your children can outrun you

The idea of running may sound horrifying, when you barely have the energy to get through the day. With the progressive introduction of gentle running, you will be surprised to find that you are actually fresher, due to your improved physical and psychological adaptation to daily life.

You would feel ridiculous out there running

You can run in discreet places to start with, until your self-esteem and confidence increases enough to get past this fear. Running will help to consolidate your confidence so that you can do what you want to do, and not what other people think you should do.

You are too old to start. If only you had thought about this 20 years ago!

Many women have started running after age 50. Some have even started a training programme after the age of 80! It is amazing but true. Age is not an insurmountable barrier. A 60 year old needs to

start out differently from a 20 year old, but that doesn't mean that she is not able to undertake a serious running/fitness programme. It is not too late.

Running was always your worst sport it hurt – and you really hate that!

Your feelings may not come from the fact that you are a poor runner, but rather from the fact that your physical education teacher had too many kids in the class to be able to help each person find his or her comfortable pace. If you were required to run harder than you should have, no wonder you felt incompetent. We are going to look at a personalised, self-paced programme that will suit you well, and that will be based on the idea of *gentle* exertion, not pain.

You prefer team sports

Team sports are great, there is no doubt about that. The advantage that you might find in running is the fact that as life gets busy, the more 'portable' the sport, the more likely you are to participate. If you have to depend on others, if you have to reserve a court, if you have to pay fees to participate, you will have more factors to organise if you want to keep a fitness programme going.

Running, on the other hand, lets you be the boss. You can do it when and where you want to. It is also an excellent base for all sports, so that the time you spend running will contribute to improving your tennis (basketball, softball...) game!

You are too fat to run

All good running programmes for unfit beginners start with walking first, then provide a transition to running. With advice from a qualified medical professional, you *can* run, and running will help you to bring your weight down, and feel more comfortable in your daily activities.

Sarah R. (43, artist)

Running was proving to myself that I could do something that I couldn't do when I was much younger. In the beginning, I'd run between telephone poles and then stop. I quickly discovered that I could carry on running and that if I had to stop, all I had to do was to run more slowly the next time. *I was running!* I was 33 when I started, and it was marvellous!

When I had children, and gave up my career, I felt like I was not contributing to society, and I felt invisible. The better I ran, the more visible I felt. Running brought me back into the world!

CHAPTER ONE

Before You Start

There are many different ways to train. Physiologists are constantly seeking to improve the training methods for attaining optimum performance. The number of options are baffling: high mileage/low intensity, low mileage/high intensity, resistance training/high intensity, and on and on... There will always be new schools of thought, and revitalisation of old ones. Runners continue to learn and succeed as they follow the training advice of Arthur Lydiard, running guru of the sixties and seventies. Leading sports scientist and runner Tim Noakes looks to the training of Arthur Newton, world record holder and champion runner during the 1920s and 1930s, for inspired training programmes of the 1990s! Running magazines regularly proclaim: *Run faster in four weeks! No Pain, No Gain! Marathon Success Guaranteed (six-step programme)! World's Best Peaking programme!*[1]

No one knows the absolute truth concerning the 'best' possible way to train, probably because the lifestyles, health conditions, climatic and geographical situation of each individual are so different. There is no magic recipe that everyone can follow. That is why it is so important for each woman to know where she wants to go, to be aware of her own strengths and weaknesses, and to be willing to learn enough about running to make decisions about what is most likely to work for her. What might be good at one point in her running career might alter drastically at another time due to changes in fitness, in health, or in family life. This is probably more true for women than for men, due to often heavier work loads (domestic and professional), pregnancy, motherhood and in some cases inferior levels of fitness prior to starting exercise.

---

1 Genuine titles taken from reputable running journals.

Women need flexible training programmes which can adjust to their needs. Recognising your own needs, identifying your personal strengths and weaknesses, defining your motivational impetus are perhaps just as important in the success of your running or fitness programme as the actual training plan! With these thoughts in mind, it is clear that a recipe book approach to running would not fit the needs of most women. On the other hand, there are some elements which are essential in order for any programme to be successful, and which can be seen as universal to all training philosophies. They have nothing to do with the programmes themselves, but with the way that you use them. Remember the golden rules in all that you do, and get ready to run!

DEFINE YOUR GOALS

You have to know where you want to go in order to get there. Give it some serious thought. Do you want to improve your baseline fitness? Lose a pound or two (or even more)? Run the ten-kilometre road race held in your town every October, or perhaps finish a marathon? Qualify for the national championships or just break six minutes for the mile? Or simply reintegrate physical activity into your daily life? All of these goals are valid, and each will meet the needs of some women. In order to succeed, you need to think about what *you* would like running to give to you. Write down that goal somewhere (your training log, which we will discuss further on, will be the perfect place to record your goal), and you are already well on your way to success. Without a goal, you have no way to monitor your training. You cannot give yourself positive reinforcement because you have no way to evaluate your progress.

Keep your goals within reason. They must be achievable. Committing yourself to running a marathon in one month would be beyond the ability of even a very fit beginner! It is better to be cautious, than overly ambitious, at this stage. Ask for help in setting your goals from a friend who runs, or from a coach or physical education instructor. If you can, ask someone who has experience and who knows you well. Do they think you are biting off more than you can chew? Re-evaluate your goal. On the other hand, if they feel you are being too cautious, don't be too quick to intensify your training programme. There will be time to re-assess along the way. The danger of over-estimation is much greater than that of setting too modest a goal.

CHECK WITH YOUR DOCTOR

You should see your doctor every year, whether you run or not. It is much better for her or him to know you well, so that if you should become ill, or have health problems, they needn't make your acquaintance in the middle of a crisis. It is to your advantage as well to know and trust the person who guides you in sickness and in health. If you have not seen your doctor in over a year, if you have been leading a sedentary life for more than a year or two, if you have been smoking or drinking heavily, or if there is any history of heart disease in your family, it is imperative for you to see your physician before you undertake a running programme. Remember: prevention is always the best treatment, and this consultation with your doctor will help to rule out any cardiac or physical problems which could affect your programme. Furthermore, your doctor is likely to become an enthusiastic advocate for your efforts, and that kind of support is helpful.

KEEP A RECORD:
The Training Diary

The training diary is very helpful for a beginning runner. Writing down what you have done over the course of the day can in itself be relaxing and satisfying. Most of us have memories of the diaries we kept as girls. Reading over them again, years later, can be an eye-opening experience. So many things escape our memories if we don't jot them down on

	Date	Mood	Dist	Time	Comments
M					
T					
W					
T					
F					
S					
S					
Weekly total					

Figure 1: Weekly training record

a piece of paper. The running or training diary can serve the same role. Not only does it remind you of your commitment, it will also jog your memory of past training experiences. This is valuable when you want to think back on what worked and what didn't. It is encouraging as well, because some days, when you are frustrated or tired, you can look back and see where you have come from, and how much you have improved over the previous weeks and months, even if that particular day wasn't so hot.

You can use a notebook, a weekly or monthly planner, a computer programme, or a specially designed runner's diary. Runner's diaries are available at sports stores, book stores, and through most mail order sports-supply companies. What should you record in your diary?

For now, just writing down your name and your current goals on the front page will be helpful. It is a sign of the commitment you are making to your own well-being and happiness. Even if no one else ever looks at a single page of your diary, it is as if you had someone else looking over your shoulder, keeping track of what you are up to, and how you are doing.

You will use the training diary as a reminder. It helps you to recall the intensity of your runs (fast, easy), and the duration. After each run, take a few minutes to write down the important details: the duration of the run, the course, how you felt, heart rate at the end of your run, any change of rhythm, or speed work incorporated in the run, and the distance (if known). Three weeks down the track, when you can't understand why you are so tired, you can take a look back, and maybe get a clue as to how the problem began. The training diary can also help provide encouragement. 'Last year, when I ran that same circuit, I puffed through in 32 minutes. Yesterday, I did it in 28, and felt easy the whole way!' It provides a record of what worked for you, or of what left you tired and wanting to throw in the towel.

I use my running diaries to motivate myself. I love to compare work-outs to see if I have improved, but I also love graphing my mileage, plotting my goals, and simply writing little narratives about runs I have particularly enjoyed. It is fun to read back over them. There was one day, running on the Appalachian trail near my parents' weekend hideaway in the Blue Ridge Mountains, that I bumped into a baby bear! I have recorded that moment in my diary. I use this little book to write down my wildest dreams of accomplishment. Once I have dared to write down a time I hope to achieve over the course of the season, for example, I feel a bit more capable of attaining it.

You can photocopy Figure 1 for your personal use, if you wish. This is the format I use to record my running and sporting activities. You will note that there is a column for 'mood'. I rate my mood on a five point scale: 5 – very high, 4 – high, 3 – okay, 2 – low, and 1 – the

pits. It can be helpful to record your mood, and measure the highs and lows, as mood is one of the first things likely to change when you are training more than you should.

DRESS TO RUN

RUNNING SHOES

Your training shoes have the important responsibility of protecting your feet, and your entire musculoskeletal system, from the jarring produced at each stride. With every mile, your feet hammer the ground more than 1700 times. 1700 times, your joints bounce and bump up and down, up and down. A good pair of shoes will protect you from injury, and provide you with comfort during your training runs. Tennis shoes are designed for quick lateral movement, and basketball shoes are designed to help you jump, and to stabilise the ankle. A running shoe, on the other hand, is designed to protect you from the road, correct possible bio-mechanical problems, and stabilise your foot strike. The purchase of a good running shoe is the only important investment you need make.

How do I choose a good running shoe?

First, find a store which is known to be interested in runners and athletes. You will need good advice, and the local bargain basement is not the place to get that. There is no 'best' shoe. You will need to find what is suited to your foot, your body type, your training speed and mileage. A good sales person with experience in the needs of runners will help to guide you. Keep the following thoughts in mind, however.

How much do I need to spend?

Prices vary enormously, but the best shoe for you is not necessarily the most expensive one. On principle, I buy only reasonably priced shoes. Don't forget that the running shoe market has been evolving rapidly, and last year's models are still fine for a beginning runner. The research laboratories of all the major running shoe companies are aggressively developing and promoting new features, designed to improve comfort, performance, or the life of the sole. The promotion of such technical improvements, however, is designed to improve the annual report to shareholders. So, if your budget is limited, avoid the newest improvements, and settle for a good, but less expensive shoe. But be sure to choose a shoe from a reputable and established running shoe manufacturer, which benefits from such scientific research.

Which model is for you?

For a beginner who doesn't plan (for the moment, at least) on arduous training,

> J. D. (32, teacher)
>
> I couldn't believe what a new pair of shoes did for my running. I feel like I only have to run half as hard as I did with the old beat-up ones. It is as if they are taking half of the strides for me!

or high mileage, the most important factor is to find a model which stabilises the foot adequately, and which provides good shock absorption. The shoe should be adapted to your foot strike. You may **pronate**. This means that as your heel strikes the ground, and you prepare to push off again, your foot rolls to the inside. If you pronate, you may note that there is more sole wear on the inside of the heel or the forefoot on a well-worn pair of your shoes. On the other hand, you may **supinate**, which means that you shift your weight to the outside of your foot as you prepare for each new stride. This is seen by wear on the outside of the sole. Shoes can be specifically designed for the type of foot strike you demonstrate, be it supination or pronation. The goal is to correctly *stabilise* your foot strike to avoid excessive strain on your legs. You may also have a biomechanically efficient foot, and require less stabilisation, in which case a corrective shoe would not feel comfortable at all, and would affect your gait. This is why an experienced running shoe advisor will be important to you.

In addition to your foot strike, you must also examine your cushioning needs. If you carry any extra weight right now, if you will be running primarily on hard surfaces, or if you have quite small feet (smaller surface area for shock absorption), you will need a highly cushioned and protective shoe. There are many technical means for adding cushioning to a shoe: air inserts, honey-comb energy absorption designs, gel pockets and so on. Remember, extra cushioning increases comfort, but adds to the weight of the shoe.

Is your foot rigid, or floppy? My feet hit the ground a bit like boards. If I put them in a stiff pair of training shoes, it accentuates my defect, and slap! slap! slap! – you can hear me pounding the pavement for miles! I need a flexible training shoe, whereas a friend with high arches may do better to have the control offered by a board lasted shoe.

Is a curved or straight last better suited to your foot? A straight lasted shoe is exactly as its name suggests, straight. If you drew a line on the sole from the middle of the toe to the middle of the heel, it would be perfectly straight. Curve lasted shoes will have a banana shaped arc to the sole. The straight last helps to prevent pronation, while the curve last allows more foot movement, and is best suited to bio-mechanically efficient runners.

Obviously, the myriad of choices to be made reflects the fact that there is no one 'best' shoe, and that once presented with the shoes which suit your needs, you still need to feel comfortable once the shoe is on your foot. Try on several pairs. Your foot should feel well balanced and comfortable. You should feel naturally at ease, and as you take a step or two, your foot should not feel repositioned, or shifted. Some stores will let you take a few running strides on the footpath, or down a carpeted hallway. Take advantage of that option to judge the shoe's suitability to your stride.

What size is right?

You may need one half size longer than your regular shoe size. Your feet may swell as you run, and there must be space for that. A well-fitted shoe will give you a thumb's width between the tip of the longest toe, and the end of the shoe's upper. Different lacing techniques can adjust the tightness of the shoe across the top. Consult the sales person, or an experienced runner for advice.

If your feet do tend to swell, make sure to shop for your running shoes in the afternoon, when they are more swollen, or at the time of day that you expect to run.

What about men's shoes?

We have come a long way in the domain of women's footwear for running. I am blessed with a big foot, which means I have been able to wear men's shoes. This is a great advantage, as it means that the entire array of technical advances are available to me. To wear men's footwear however, I have to put up with a shoe which is usually too wide, or too heavy. My legs are exhausted from having to lug around a shoe designed for a man 4 stone heavier than me. So, thank heavens for women's running shoes! They cover the range of women's foot sizes, starting at size three and a half and moving up, and they provide a snugger, better adapted fit. As the women's market is smaller, however, there is still a similarly smaller range of models available for women from each shoe company than for men.

If you don't find what you want in women's shoes, and if your foot can fit in a man's sized shoe, try the men's models. They may not come in pastel shades, but they will offer more of the features which you require.

How often should I buy new shoes?

New shoes provide optimum protection, which will decline progressively over the life of the shoe. An experienced runner will immediately examine his or her shoes for signs of wear at the first ache or pain in any joint or muscle. Often, when it seems to take more time for the legs to spring back after hard runs, or when little niggles crop up in the feet or legs, you can look back to your shoes, and discover that they have, indeed, done their job, and are ready to be replaced. Always record the wearing of new shoes in your training diary. Usually, a good pair of running shoes will last for many hundreds of miles. But there are exceptions to this rule. A heavy runner, or one with a very unstable foot-strike, will need to change shoes more often. To lengthen the life of the shoes, reserve them for training alone, and keep a pair of tennis shoes for kick-around activities.

Where else can I get advice?

All of the major running magazines in America and Europe, do a yearly running shoe review. Often the information contained in the surveys is promotional, but they do point out the strengths of each brand and/or model. Often, editorial comment or evaluation helps to clarify further. Save the shoe survey issue, for once you know what your shoe preferences are, you can use it to extend your selection. I like a light weight, slip form, curve lasted, minimally cushioned training shoe which suits a narrow foot. When I am on the market for new shoes, I can look down the comparative charts and see which models have the features I need.

Seek advice from experienced runners you may know. But, remember, what suits them may or may not suit you. The most important advice they will give you is 'Oh! You should go see Todd, at Running Shoe Warehouse,[2] he's got good prices, and he knows his shoes!'

CLOTHING

One of the nice things about running is that you don't need fancy clothing. No cute pleated white skirts, no padded shorts, just something comfortable to move freely about in will do. The only truly important article of clothing is the training shoe. Good clothes won't make you run any faster, but poorly suited clothing can make the experience much less fulfilling (and sometimes even downright uncomfortable!).

Shorts, pants and the like

First of all, remember that you need to feel good about how you look. It's easy to feel discouraged. If you are wearing clothes that are badly cut, or emphasise all the little lumps and bulges of which you are self-conscious (even if, as we will discuss at length further on, they are perfectly normal and no one else may even notice them!), you will feel less confident running. Instead of buying the first pair of shorts on the rack, look until you find some which make you feel

comfortable. They should be non-binding, loose fitting, and with smooth seams which will not chafe between the legs. Some of the synthetic fabrics have the added advantage of wicking away moisture, be it rain, or perspiration, whereas cotton is softer, but more absorbent, and so often chafes. It is a purely personal choice as to what you choose to wear. The silky feeling of lycra tights may make one person feel set to fly, but may convey a painful feeling of nudity to another. Figure 2 may help you to sort things out for yourself.

BREAST SUPPORT
– the running bra

The breast – symbol of femininity, of motherhood, of sensuality – can get in the way when you run. Whether you are slim or chunky, small-breasted or 'busty', your breasts will move when you run, and choosing proper breast support is quite important to your comfort.

Running will not make your breasts sag, no matter how large they may be. The breast is made of glandular tissue, enclosed in an adipose envelope, surrounded by ligaments and skin. The glandular tissue is separated into lobes which are drained by ducts when milk is secreted. Breast size varies, as we know, from one woman to another. The individual size of breasts changes with the hormonal fluctuation of menstrual

---

2 Fictitious names.

Item	What to look for	Recommended use	Advantages	Disadvantages
briefs	Avoid high cut on the legs. They will ride up when you run.	competition of short duration	• no binding • makes you look 'hot', possibly useful for psyching out the competition	• does not prevent chafing between thighs, which is common in runners, especially female
shorts	Choose shorts with a built-in brief, which dispenses with the need for panties, and reduces binding.	training or racing	• gives freedom of movement to the legs	• does not eliminate all chafing
un-padded bike shorts	lycra, or lycra cotton blends are desirable. Make sure that there is a cotton-lined gusset at the crotch so you don't have to wear panties. Also, make sure that the elastic, or hem, at the leg is not restrictive.	training or racing	• shiny and smooth, it makes you feel very aerodynamic • it stretches in all directions, so does not bind at all • it eliminates all chafing between the legs	• may be intimidating for a woman who is not accustomed to seeing herself in sports clothes • not subtle
tights	Lycra, cotton Lycra blends or thermal fabrics for winter climates.	training or racing in low temperatures	same as bike shorts	same as bike shorts
sweatsuit	Preferably made in absorbent fabric, or lined with such.	training	• covers and warms up the entire leg • discreet	• bulkier than the above mentioned items • heavier, especially when wet

Figure 2: Choosing your clothing

> **Julie W.**
> (37, single mother, three children)
>
> It is so much less expensive than other sports! I had been involved in aerobics, but it was costing me so much, and my budget was really tight. I can just walk out the door and go for a run whenever I like.

cycles, pregnancy, lactation and menopause. With age, the bottom half of the breast often loses its round form, which makes the breast appear to sag. Can the jostling of running contribute to the sagging? No! According to Joan Ullyot, MD, and experienced runner/writer, 'Breasts are supported mainly by their own content of glands and fat. "Sagging" occurs because of age and hormonal changes, which reduce this supportive filling. Sports are not the culprit.'[3] Dr Ullyot states that we can even run without a bra if we so desire.

The problem is a little more tricky than this. If you have large breasts, you know that their bobbing up and down can cause discomfort when you run. The possibility of catcalls and harassment when running without adequate breast support makes things worse.

The running bra market has exploded with the advent of strong female participation in long-distance

running and aerobics. New fabrics are perfectly adapted to these garments. Adieu to the underwire and hooks, which used to torture our fragile skin as we pioneered the women's running movement before the clothing manufacturers caught up with our needs! Many of us bear scars where those same underwires (at the time, the only support available) chafed and dug. Today there are choices, offering comfort and support, which far exceed that of the traditional brassiere.

Features of good breast support
Support
Support is determined both by design, and by the textile used in making the top. To decrease the vertical movement of the breasts (the up-and-down bobbing), the textile used must have minimal vertical elasticity. To further prevent the bobbing, the breasts must also be drawn closer to the centre of gravity by a top which has a 'flattening' effect. This distributes the breast mass across the chest, and encourages them to move *with* the body, instead of in opposition, as occurs when there is bobbing. Large-breasted women may not be able to wear a flattening shape, but can choose a sport bra with cups which are designed to control motion.

Support is also determined by the degree to which the top is anchored,

---

3 Joan Ullyot, *Running Free*, Perigree Books, 1980, pages 186–7.

Characteristic	Seek	Rule out
Support	• flattening cut • soft comfortable fabric	• pointed cups • fabrics with excessive vertical elasticity • stretchy straps
Comfort	• vented panels • strap design to your taste • flat, well-finished seams • one-piece design	• inadequate support • poorly finished or poorly located seams (none should cross the nipple area) • fussy, lacy details • hooks, eyes, metal or plastic closures

Figure 3: What to look for in a running top

both above and below the breasts. Running bras are usually much wider than a traditional bra for that reason.

Comfort

Aside from support, there are additional features which further enhance the degree of comfort. Highly supportive textiles do not necessarily 'breathe' well, so vented panel insets are welcome. The bra straps may affect comfort, and come in many styles: crossed, traditional, or racerback. The straps must not allow up and down movement, nor should they have abrasive seams or lace. All of the seams should be flat and smooth. Beware of seams across the mid cup, as they can be irritating when running. Hooks and eyes, as well as any metal closures should be avoided for the same reason.

My skin is very delicate, and I find that I often benefit by wearing my bras inside out when I run so as to have the finished side of the seam against my skin, rather than the more ragged inside seam.

Remember that the risk of chafing is increased when the skin is damp, as when perspiring.

Running Bras

There is a great array of running and action tops available but the important thing is finding the top which best suits your needs. You may not need much support, but have particularly sensitive skin. You may like your top to look really flash, so that you can wear it without a singlet in warm weather. If you have a large bust, you will undoubtedly want firm support.

MISCELLANEOUS EQUIPMENT

I won't contradict myself by saying that there is anything else you need for running. Remember, all we need are our legs and a pair of shoes. If you are into gadgets, or if your purse is well-filled, there are a few more items that might tickle your fancy, or improve your comfort. Here goes!

Socks: Look for socks which fit snugly, as any gathering or bunching will create blisters. Seams should be smooth. If your feet perspire heavily, look for fabrics that 'wick' the moisture away from the foot (and increase the price of the sock).

Stopwatch: A digital watch with a stopwatch function is terrific for timing your runs and work-outs. I have always felt that the fluorescent watch bands make me run faster, so obviously they are a good marketing device (just kidding, they are actually just prettier). Models with a memory can store a minute-record of your runs which is an attractive feature if you forget to write them down in your diary. But generally you won't need a 30-lap memory, or split timing capacity unless you turn into a serious competitor, so a simple model will do.

Wind jacket: We will discuss the features of cold weather gear in chapter four. Refer to those pages for more information about various fabrics which can improve your comfort in inclement weather.

Sunglasses: UV protection for your eyes is desirable. Those 'hot' looking wrap-around sport glasses are actually a terrific invention. I spent more money than I like to say on a pair about five years ago, and they go with me everywhere. They are light, do not ride up on my nose or bob, and make running in bright conditions much easier. They are a bit hard on the purse, however.

Thermal wear: In areas where the weather can change without a second's notice, and where the wind and rain can be devastatingly cold, a thermal top and bottom is useful. You needn't go and buy something new if you already have thermal wear for the winter. The important thing is to have warm enough clothing that a grotty winter day doesn't dissuade you from exercising. If you decide to exercise only when the weather is clement, you will miss too much good conditioning!

Bum bag: I don't like running with a bum bag, but I know how helpful it is to have one for those times when I *must* carry small items with me on my run. If I am going off-road or for a long run, some snacks, or even a water bottle may be necessary. A telephone card, a pound or two and the car keys may be necessary but can be cumbersome if you have to carry them in your hand, or have them smack around in the pocket of your jacket.

Emergency blanket: Thank heavens I haven't had to use it yet, but I do own one of those silver-coated emergency blankets. Just imagine going for a run in the country on a brisk autumn day, when the temperature is hovering around ten degrees. You are five miles from home when you turn your ankle while watching a bird. The wind has changed by that time, and it is starting to rain. What is more, you are already a bit sweaty, and your clothes are drenched. It is going to be a long hobble back to the car! That is when the emergency blanket, which weighs less than an ounce, will be a helpful addition to your paraphernalia list.

Heart monitor: These are monitors which you wear on your wrist, like a digital stopwatch. They can be quite helpful to a serious runner, or triathlete, who has access to physiological testing. They can help you to determine the exact level of exertion which is required for a specific session. Although they are a brilliant addition to the training equipment list of the serious runner, they are not necessary for most.

Sun hat: A baseball-style cap is a good idea for a runner. Runners get more sun exposure than most, and wearing a cap is a good way of keeping the UV rays off your face and ears. Furthermore, such caps are perfect for running in the rain. They keep the water from running down your face. If you have a water-repellent cap for running in the rain, don't make the mistake of wearing it on a hot, sunny run, because you will overheat beneath it. So, have a light-coloured, non-waterproof sun cap, and a waterproof cap for rainy days.

Sunscreen: Don't forget that an hour running is an hour in the sun! Slap on some sunscreen for midsummer, or midday runs.

PHYSIOLOGY OF RUNNING
JUST A PEEK

A Heart Which Beats For You

You don't need to be a physiologist in order to run. Far from it! On the other hand, if you have a basic understanding of what your body is actually doing when you run, you will be able to make better choices about your training, because you will understand the signals your body is sending.

Sixty to seventy times a minute, one hundred thousand times a day, and more than thirty-five million times a year, your heart beats, sending blood to all the parts of the body. Seen as the centre of the soul, the seat of all emotion, personality and spirituality, the heart is indeed the life centre of the body. It makes the blood circulate, allowing oxygen and nutrients to go to the tissues which need them. It also helps to cleanse the body, delivering metabolic and gaseous end products to those organs which will remove them from the body.

The heart is a muscle which must contract in order to pump. With each beat or contraction of this mighty muscle, the left ventricle ejects relatively highly oxygenated blood into the aorta. The arterial network then delivers this blood to the tissues. On the other side of the heart, the right ventricle delivers its contents, which is venous blood, containing higher levels of CO_2, to the lungs. There, the gases are exchanged, with a release of the carbonic wastes, and renewed saturation of the blood with oxygen which will then be utilised by the body.

The role of the heart in running is pretty obvious. If you try to run to catch a bus, you'll realise that right away. Once you catch the bus, you will feel your heart hammering away loudly, instead of the regular boom boom that you barely notice in other circumstances. The resting heart is discreet, but as soon as you increase your activity level by running after a bus, climbing stairs, playing tennis, or being scared or upset, the heart will change pace as well. This pick-up is the result of signs from other parts of the body, such as the muscles requiring the heart/motor to pump harder.

To run, dance, climb the stairs, or jump, we must use our muscles. Muscle contraction is what makes us move. Muscles need oxygen in order to contract quickly over a sustained period of time, as when you perform any of the above activities. The heart beats faster to distribute more oxygen to the muscles which need it. This is particularly true of running, because the muscles need lots of oxygen to keep going, and likewise, need to eliminate the carbon dioxide waste by the other side of the heart pump. During exercise, heart rate can be as much as three or four times what it is at rest. As the heart rate increases, the volume of blood ejected with each beat gets bigger and cardiac output[4] increases to levels which can be as much as six times the resting output!

What is it that keeps us from running further, or faster? You can probably remember the feeling: your chest on fire, legs burning, intolerable shortness of breath, and a heart beating so fast you

---

4 Cardiac output = heart rate x volume of blood ejected with each beat.

think you might explode. Those feelings are certainly enough to dissuade you from continuing to exercise. What has happened is that the muscles' oxygen requirement has surpassed the heart and lungs' capacity to supply it, and the muscles' ability to use it. As a result, there is a reduction in the available energy, as well as a build-up of metabolic end products, such as CO_2 and lactic acid. The presence of these elements is a sign that the energy need is greater than the ability of the body to satisfy it aerobically (using oxygen). The build-up of waste products lowers the blood pH, making it more acidic, and creating the horrible symptoms described above. At this stage, the heart beats furiously to try to eliminate the excess carbon dioxide, and bring in more oxygen, but in vain. When you feel like this, you will be very close to throwing in the towel.

Steady state aerobic activity, unlike the exercise described above, will be well tolerated for a long time, because there will be balance between supply and demand which will not lead to those painful feelings. The interesting thing is that we have some ability to extend our individual limits, postponing the arrival of what is often referred to as the 'anaerobic threshold' or the 'lactate turnpoint' – the point at which we go beyond the steady state. If running made you feel as badly as I have described above, well, nobody would

ever want to run! The goal of training is to help the body to operate efficiently, and as long as possible, below that threshold. We want to teach our bodies how to run faster, without feeling exhausted. For example, today, if you were to go out and run one mile in seven minutes, you might be pushing yourself to your most extreme limit. But, after a few weeks of good training, you might feel very good at that same speed – barely winded, ready to continue. This would signify that you have succeeded in extending your aerobic capacity. That is the point of the training you are about to undertake: training your body to run faster and further, with less effort.

SO, WHY WORRY ABOUT CARDIAC PHYSIOLOGY?

You can use this understanding of the way the heart works to help you evaluate the intensity of your running programme. To succeed in a running programme, it is vital to work hard enough (but not too hard), run fast enough (but not too fast), and to see how the body is responding to the work it is doing. If you are not yet an experienced runner, however, it is sometimes difficult to tell just how much is enough. Monitoring your heart rate can help. You want to be able to train below your anaerobic threshold, although sometimes you might want to train quite close to the edge.

Because it is much easier to count the heart rate than it is to measure the blood lactic acid and CO_2 (this can only be done by drawing blood and putting it through expensive laboratory machines), researchers have attempted to establish the relationship between the heart rate and blood lactic acid. As you might imagine, the heart rate climbs rapidly when you start getting close to the lactate turnpoint. There is a close relationship between heart rate and oxygen uptake, so the heart rate can tell us a great deal about the intensity of our aerobic work. This information is helpful, since you can take your own pulse, or heart rate. You can then, using your pulse, as well as the way you are feeling, decide if the

intensity of your training is right. Once you become familiar with the feelings associated with various ranges of heart rate, you will be able to judge your level of exertion without actually taking your pulse. But, to start with, let's actually count the heartbeats.

HOW TO TAKE YOUR PULSE

To take your pulse, you simply apply light pressure with your fingertips to an easily accessible artery, such as the radial, or subclavian arteries. You'll find the radial artery on the thumb side of your wrist, or the subclavian in the notch above your breastbone. With the second hand of your watch, or with your stopwatch, count the number of beats you feel over a 15-second period. Multiply that number by four to obtain your pulse for one minute. This may take some practice, and you may initially count too few, or too many beats. As you practice, you will improve your ability to count.

Resting heart rate

Take your pulse right now. If you are sitting comfortably, and are calm and well rested, you will be measuring your resting pulse. One of the best times to obtain your resting heart rate, and to know that it is truly a reflection of your heart at rest, is right before you go to

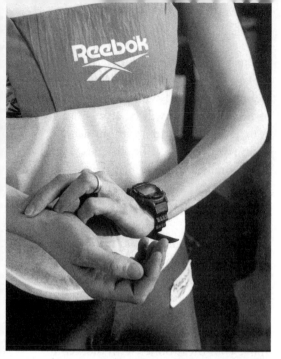

heart rate is simply one element of a much bigger picture.

The heart rate and exercise

As a beginner, you will be most interested in your heart rate during exercise, mainly because it can help to keep you running at the right pace. If you run too fast in the beginning, you will not improve, because you will not give yourself the proper aerobic base on which all the rest of your training must be built. You want to train in a target zone, which is under your anaerobic threshold. Your own special target zone may be different from someone else's. It depends on your age and your level of fitness. Figure 4 provides you with approximate heart rates for your target zone, based on your age. A physiologist could give you more precise numbers, after extensive testing, but in most cases this is an adequate guide for your purposes.

sleep at night. If you have been lying down for ten or fifteen minutes, thumbing through a magazine, or reading, you will probably find that your pulse is at its slowest at that time. The resting pulse of a well-trained runner is likely to be slower than that of most people, because the runner's heart is capable of ejecting more blood with each beat. Its pumping chambers (the ventricles) are larger, and its pumping force is greater. Some people use the measurement of the resting heart beat to evaluate whether or not they are getting fitter from their running. Resting heart rates vary from person to person. Just having a slow heart rate does not mean you are fit, nor does having a quick one mean you are at death's door. Resting

After your run, your heart rate should not be above or below the highlighted zone. Ideally, it should be somewhere right in the middle. When you get quite proficient at taking your pulse, you should count for only ten seconds, and multiply by six, to get a more accurate idea of the pulse rate at the end of the run. This is because you are taking your pulse when you stop exercising, and it will naturally slow down, especially if you are very fit. You want to 'catch' your pulse as quickly as you can at the end of your run, before it has a chance to change pace significantly. If your heart rate is in the high range, or outside of the zone, you should slow down your running, because it shows that you are probably exercising at an intensity which is too high to benefit you at this time. Slowing your pace will slow your heart rate. If you feel good, but your pulse is too high, find an experienced person to verify your pulse with you. It may be that you have counted an extra beat or two. That is a common mistake, given the speed at which your heart fires during exercise. If your heart rate is below the recommended zone, get someone to check your pulse with you. You may have missed a few beats. Do not necessarily pick up the pace as yet. Just settle in, and use your feelings of exertion as a guide. If you remain lower than the recommended zone, pay a call on your doctor, and ask for advice.

Recovery heart rate

You can tell a lot about how your body is responding to exercise by the way your

age	Exercise Heart Rate											
20			100	110	120	130	140	150	160	170	180	190
25			100	110	120	130	140	150	160	170	180	190
30		90	100	110	120	130	140	150	160	170	180	190
35		90	100	110	120	130	140	150	160	170	180	190
40		90	100	110	120	130	140	150	160	170	180	190
45	80	90	100	110	120	130	140	150	160	170	180	190
50	80	90	100	110	120	130	140	150	160	170	180	
55	80	90	100	110	120	130	140	150	160	170	180	
60	80	90	100	110	120	130	140	150	160	170		
65	80	90	100	110	120	130	140	150	160	170		
70	80	90	100	110	120	130	140	150	160	170		

Figure 4: Target exercise heart rate: The highlighted zone provides you with a general indication of where your heart rate should be during exercise, according to your age.

heart rate recovers after running. At the end of your run, you will have taken your heart rate to determine your exercise rate. One minute later (watch the clock!), take your pulse again. If all is well, and if you have not been exercising too hard, your heart rate should rapidly fall below the target zone. Take your pulse again, after three to five minutes, and you should be at fifty per cent of your theoretical maximal heart rate (see Figure 5). Once again, if your heart rate indicates that you recover too slowly, modify your pace to allow proper recovery. If you recover quickly, that's good. Your heart is responding well. You are getting fit!

The Basis for Progress

Okay; we've talked about limits, but how can you push your limits further? One principle guides all the training that you will do. You must work, then rest, if you hope to reap the benefits of the work. Let's say you want to pick up a big rock which is sitting in front of your house, but you can't budge it right now. You can go out and try to lift it every single day, but that won't help you in the long run. A better tactic would be to lift a smaller rock for practice. You could lift a smaller rock which is close to the current limit of your strength,

age	Recovery Heart Rate											
20	<60	70	80	90	100	110	120	130	140	150	160	170
25	<60	70	80	90	100	110	120	130	140	150	160	170
30	<60	70	80	90	100	110	120	130	140	150	160	170
35	<60	70	80	90	100	110	120	130	140	150	160	170
40	<60	70	80	90	100	110	120	130	140	150	160	170
45	<60	70	80	90	100	110	120	130	140	150	160	170
50	<60	70	80	90	100	110	120	130	140	150	160	170
55	<60	70	80	90	100	110	120	130	140	150	160	170
60	<60	70	80	90	100	110	120	130	140	150	160	170
65	<60	70	80	90	100	110	120	130	140	150	160	170
70	<60	70	80	90	100	110	120	130	140	150	160	170

Heart rate after 1 minute   Heart rate after 3 to 5 minutes

Figure 5: Recovery heart rate

then give your body a chance to recover from lifting it. The next time you try, you could take a slightly heavier rock. Giving yourself adequate recovery after each lift, you could progressively come to the point of lifting a heavier rock than you thought possible in the beginning. That is the principle behind all sound running programmes. If you start from a baseline level of fitness, and you work just under your limits, given proper recovery, you will be able to improve that baseline. If you don't give yourself enough rest between workouts, you will have initial improvement, followed by deterioration. The way work and rest help you to become stronger is a perfect example of how the body adapts to exercise (see Figure 6). You must always keep both components of adaptation in your training.

After all this physiological exposé, maybe the most important thing to remember when you start running is just a piece of lay wisdom: your body is the boss. Treat it properly, and listen to what it has to say. If you are attentive, it won't lead you astray.

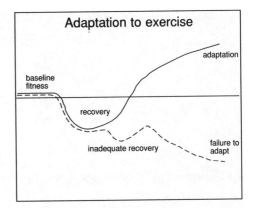

Figure 6: The solid line shows adaptation to exercise. The dotted line shows the effect of work without rest.

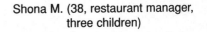

Shona M. (38, restaurant manager, three children)

It was difficult at first but it didn't take long before I started to feel fit. And enjoying it! I knew I was a runner when I couldn't wait to go out. With working full-time and having three kids, I really need my running. I want to get out every day. I think and plan things. I mainly run on my own because I like the quiet and I can go where I like. Running gives me space and freedom.

CHAPTER TWO

Starting Out

JUST HOW FIT ARE YOU?

Since I have promised to provide you with an individualised approach to running, you will first have to do some thinking about your current level of fitness. Are you a true beginner, or have you been maintaining some kind of exercise in your lifestyle, even though it might not compare to what you plan to undertake? We will try to fit you into entry levels which are based on some easy questions which you can answer yourself. If in doubt, err on the side of caution, and choose the more

conservative of the options. Likewise, if you smoke, but otherwise fit the description of one of the categories described below, take a step back and start in the previous category. Although the starting recommendations are directed at all beginners, the more closely they match your ability level, the more likely you are to succeed.

Even if you are in one of the two advanced beginner levels, read the recommendations made to the 'true beginner', as there still may be some information of use to you.

The True Beginner

You have never been athletic – that is, until you thought of taking up running. Since you left school, you have done almost no sports and only minimal outdoor activity. You don't have a physically demanding job, and the most athletic thing you remember doing

---

Muriel H. (51)

I talk to people who are a lot younger than I am, and they're not fit. They always seem to have something wrong with them. They get a lot of colds, and are run-down, even if they're only in their forties. I am just leaps ahead of them by keeping my fitness up!

---

recently was a Sunday stroll after dinner. Perhaps you smoke now, or once did:

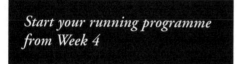

Start your running programme from Week 1

The Advanced Beginner

Your job is physically demanding, or maybe you play tennis, or bike to work once or twice a week. You pay attention to what you eat, and you do not smoke:

Start your running programme from Week 4

The Athletic Beginner

You may not be a runner, but you are physically active. You do some other kind of exercise very regularly (as much as two to three times a week, most weeks) or your job uses your physical endurance and agility and, of course, you have never smoked:

Start your running programme from Week 6

Now that you have identified the fitness level at which you should start running, let us look at the programme.

STARTING TO TRAIN

Week 1

Decide when you are going to start your running programme. Plan at least three weeks ahead of time so that you can get ready. 'Making a date' will enhance your resolve. Try to find one or two friends to join you, because it will make things a lot easier. Many a runner has started because someone else thought to invite them out. Don't assume that they will not be interested. It is much more motivating to share the first steps with a friend, but if there is none to be found, don't worry, your friends will be so impressed by your endeavour, and your new-found fitness, that they will soon be clamouring to join in! In the meantime, pick up a running magazine, and read through an article or two, or look at the pictures and motivate yourself by the example of toned and fit runners. (Oh, by the way, remember not to fall for the 'get fit in six easy steps!' or related poppycock which you may encounter in such, otherwise serious, magazines.)

Since you are a true beginner, see your doctor, or a sports doctor, to get the green light to go on with your project. Even an apparently healthy woman can have hidden problems which need to be addressed before she can start running. These can be due to hereditary factors, or your previously sedentary lifestyle, but they must be ruled out before you start to run, in order to avoid serious accidents. This is particularly true of families in which there is a history of heart disease. If your doctor does not feel that you should undertake a running programme at this time, follow the advice that he or she might give you to improve your baseline fitness enough so that you can start a programme in the future. You can afford to wait a while.

If you get the doctor's okay, take advantage of this visit to ask the doctor to show you how to take your pulse, or to verify what you have been practising.

Modify your diet a bit, to start a gradual change towards nutritional balance. Your doctor can advise you on the subject, or you can follow the recommendations in chapter six.

Cut down your cigarette smoking by one cigarette a day, and write down how many you have smoked each day in your training log. That will give you a better handle on how you are doing.

Week 1 Summary

- Set your start date.
- Write it down.
- Start your training diary.
- Find some running mates.
- Make an appointment with your docto.r

Week 2

Equip yourself this week. Get some running shoes, and an outfit, if your budget allows. You are now going to start getting mentally ready to run. You should also be talking about your project with your family and friends. They will be of great help, once you get going, so enlist their support. Now, it is possible that those who you thought would be your staunchest supporters let you down by doubting your ability to carry out your running plan. Well, never you mind! You will have some friends to stand by you, but mainly, you will have your own resolve, which I will do my best to strengthen as we work through this programme together.

Even though we are not yet down to running, you need to start to adjust little things in your lifestyle which will make running easier. Don't be in too big a hurry. This is going to be a long-term commitment you are making for yourself, and that is why you need to have a careful preparation to ensure your success.

Week 2 is when you start getting active. Walk whenever you get a chance, and make those chances where you hadn't thought it possible. If you use public transport, get off the bus or train one stop earlier to give your legs the time to stretch and get used to a bit of activity. Don't take the car for a little errand; instead, walk on down to the nearest shop. Take the stairs, instead of the lift, or get off a few flights early. If your lifestyle, or your work clothes (high-heeled shoes, or uncomfortable clothing) get in the way of this kind of energising, set aside a few minutes every other day to just walk briskly around the block a time or two. And finally, this week, start planning your running programme.

Planning your running

When your run becomes a habitual activity, planned far in advance, it is much easier to stick to your programme. It is a little bit like brushing your teeth. You may be in a hurry to get to work, or off on a trip, but you always find time to brush. It would make you feel like something was missing, were you to neglect that daily ritual! Well, running can become that same kind of habit.

If you have a regular schedule, you should plan when you are going to run. That way, when you get home from work after an intellectually, emotionally or physically draining day, you will be less likely to droop into the first chair you see. If you know that Tuesday and Thursday (for example) are your running days, you will keep your energy up, as you will be looking further than that silly armchair. On the other hand, if you simply think, 'Well, I am going to run three times this week – it can just as easily be tomorrow as today,' you are likely to end up in that armchair!

This may seem a bit hard, or unrealistic. It isn't really. Running won't make you tired in the way that a hard day at work or with the kids will. Au contraire! Running will give you a kind of 'second wind' after a tiring day. Take a look at your monthly planner, and see what would fit into your schedule. If you have physically demanding work, you work night shift, or you change shifts, you may have to set up a schedule which is different depending on the changes in your work schedule. When I work night shift (alas, all too frequently for my taste!) I continue to run regularly, but much less, and much more slowly. I roll out of bed about an hour before the children come home from school, and slowly plod through a gentle run. It is this habitual approach which prevents me from just saying 'Pooh!' and turning over and going back to sleep. I am much more alert, patient, and happy if I do take that run than I would be if I didn't. I cut back my training, but I don't give up when work impinges on everything else.

Decide when you are going to run, which days will be your 'training' days, and write them down. If you are planning on running three to four times a week, it is best to spread those days out over the week.

Week 2 Summary

- Get your running shoes and any additional equipment you desire and can afford.

- Broadcast your plans! Talk about them with friends and family.

- Start walking whenever you get a chance, or create the chances!

- Plan your running dates and times.

- Continue to strive for a more balanced diet (no, I did not say 'start a diet'! See references to diet and weight loss in chapter six).

Weeks 3–4

Now, get those shoes on your feet, and keep walking! You will go on with the walks around the block, but now, you'll do it with fancy new training shoes, and with intent. This is the beginning of your training. You will start, not with running, but with vigorous walking. Walk briskly. You will need to find a pace which has you working, but which does not exhaust you. You are not to run at this stage. Try walking briskly for 20 minutes two times during the week.

On the weekend, take your walk further, and try to go for a good 45 minutes. At the end of your walk, take your pulse. You will note that it increases with the intensity of the exercise. Write about these walks in your training log. Where did you go?

How long did you walk? What was your pulse rate at the end of your exercise? How did you feel?

Weeks 3 and 4 Summary

- Start training!

- Go for vigorous walks three times a week: twice for 20 minutes, and once for 45 minutes.

- Make good use of your training log.

Week 5

Finally, it is time to start running. Before you get too excited, please hear this: you must not go out too fast! No Olympic champion ever made it to the pinnacle without patience and perseverance, and if they can't do it, we ordinary folk certainly can't either. It is much wiser to start out quietly and avoid fatigue and injury, so we make it in the long run.

Starting this week, when you go for your customary walks, toss in a few minutes of jogging. For example, walk for 5 minutes at your usual pace, then run slowly for 1 minute. Walk again for two minutes, and, once more, run for one minute. You may associate the word 'run' with gazelles and Olympians. This first run should be slow enough that you could almost keep up if you were walking really fast right next to yourself. It may feel a bit silly to run so slowly, but that is truly what is meant to happen. Run at a snail's pace to start with. Repeat the run/walk pattern for 3 minutes total running time, then finish with 5 minutes of walking at your regular pace. Your running pace should feel 'easy', and you should not be winded. If you are training with someone else, you should still be able to talk during the run segments. To achieve that intensity, your run may be no faster than a walk. Never mind! It is not ridiculous to be so slow. To be too quick, on the other hand, would have you neglecting the necessary cardio-vascular build-up required for successful running. Try taking your pulse at the end of the last run segment. It should be within the first recovery zone of the table in Figure 5. If it isn't, then your pace is too quick (pulse above the zone) or too slow (unlikely, pulse is already in the second recovery zone).

Repeat the run/walk work-out once during the week, and lengthen it on the weekend by increasing the walk time on either end, and by adding one to two additional run segments.

Week 5 Summary

- Introduce running segments into your walks. (1 minute run, 2 minute walk).

- Keep to a talking pace.

- Take your pulse.

Weeks 6–8

Did you enjoy the last week? Let's keep going, then! The principles are the same. The difference is that we will increase the length of the runs. These walk/run segments will continue to improve your aerobic capacity, while progressively introducing you to a full-scale running programme.

This week, and during the next few weeks, the running segments will increase. Try to run for 2 minutes, with a 2-minute walking recovery. Repeat this 2-min run/2-min walk one, or even two times. Go out three to four times this week for a total of 4–6 minutes running each time, with the same amount of walking time. On Saturday or Sunday, when you go for your longer outing, try to run for 3–4 full minutes twice, with 2 minutes rest between each run. Continue with a vigorous walk, before and after.

If this seems easier than pie, then after one week, increase the weekday running segments to 3, or even 4 minutes, and try to cover 5–10 minutes of continuous running on the weekend. You can also shorten the walk time to just what it takes to get your breath back, and feel quite rested again.

Weeks 6–8 Summary

- Progressively lengthen the time of your running segments, i.e., 3 minute run/ 1 minute walk.

- Go for a longer continuous run on the weekend (5–10 minutes).
- Monitor your effort. Be careful not to go too fast!
- Get used to the pace which suits you best.
- Try to meet other women runners, go to a race, read a running magazine.
- Stay motivated!

Weeks 9–11

Runs should be replacing your regular walks. These outings can involve more continuous running. Once you can run 10 minutes comfortably, walk only when you really need a break. Add a minute or two to each run, until you are able to run 20 to 30 minutes with ease.

Weeks 9–11 Summary

- Only walk to warm-up, warm-down, and when necessary during the outing.
- Reread the first weeks in your training diary. (You've come a long way, baby!)
- Write down the positive lifestyle and physical changes you can attribute to running so far.

BASIC FITNESS RUNNING REGIMEN

You have become a real runner! Slowly and surely you will replace walking with running. From now on, your outings

---

How many times a week should I run?

To obtain maximum benefit from running, and so as not to start over from the beginning each week, you should aim for three times a week minimum, for about thirty minutes. It should not be too hard to find that kind of time, especially if it is broken up into manageable half-hour portions. For a beginner, three runs a week are adequate, but for someone who would like to run in races or go further than simply getting fit, at least four to five runs would be desirable.

---

will be 'runs' not 'walks', unless you are feeling particularly sluggish on a given day, or at a given moment. Feeling too sluggish, or too often sluggish? Give it a break. No, don't stop running! Slow it down, or shorten it up, but don't cut it out. Go back a week or two, and start from there. Don't risk burnout by overdoing it.

Twice a week, you should run for 20 to 30 minutes. Your third run can be a bit more ambitious. Try to increase the duration of that run from 30 to 45 and finally 60 minutes. To achieve that, you will need to run slowly and evenly.

Are you still enjoying this? How are your legs? Are they holding up? Are your shoes still comfortable and springy? You are now spending two hours a week on your health and well-being; and should feel the effects in your daily life. This is the perfect investment in well-being and you may feel you have achieved what you set out to and simply wish to continue at this level permanently. Good for you! Keep the commitment going, and encourage others to join you.

Or, you may like to take things a step further. Now that you are truly a runner would you like to increase the number of runs a week? See if you can improve your baseline speed? Get ready for a low-key race?

Before you move on to advanced running, consult the 'troubleshooting' section which deals with many of the minor problems that you may have encountered, and may need to overcome before increasing your training.

WARMING-UP

Now, you are up and running but we still haven't talked about a warm-up. Warming-up is very important before you undertake strenuous exercise. Warming-up brings increased blood flow to the muscles which will be working, priming them for the activity they are about to embark on. It also gives the muscles a hint about what they are about to do, so that they are not sluggish when you start the main body of the exercise.

A good way to illustrate how warming-up gets you going is just to think about the first mile of any run you might go for. If you just hop off your chair, and hit the road, it is most likely that the first few strides will feel very abnormal. You will probably be short of breath, and wonder how on earth you'll be able to run at all. Generally speaking, such feelings subside rather quickly. You settle into a pace, your stride becomes more fluid, and by the end of the run, it all seems much easier than it did at the start. What happened? Your body adapted to the activity you were asking it to perform. You went from a sedentary position to an active one, and took a few minutes to make the adjustment to the increased physiological demands. You warmed-up!

You will note in the previous paragraph that I mention how important warming-up is to *strenuous* activity. If you are just going for a little jog, you may be able to dispense with a formal warm-up, because your body

38

By increasing your heart rate, you will bring the additional oxygen and nutrients which are necessary for the exercise you are about to undertake. You can do this by going for a slow jog. After jogging gently for 5 to 15 minutes (the longer period is an indication for a speed session, or a competition, and not for a beginning runner before a regular training session), you may stop and do some exercises.

Move those joints!

It is quite good to put the main running joints through their full range of motion, in preparation for the work-out. Swing your arms back and forth, as if you were exaggerating the movement employed while running. Using a tree or a wall for balance, swing each leg, with the knee bent, through its range of motion. Your knee comes up towards your chest, and your foot comes back towards your backside. Rotate each foot around and about to loosen up the ankles. Point/flex your toes to loosen up your feet, and finally, rotate your head around. The neck and shoulders are often a point of tension while running, so loosening up these muscles is important as well.

will warm itself up, as you progressively introduce the exercise (as described above). If, on the other hand, you feel as though you do require a warm-up for your daily runs, or if (as we will discuss later in the book), you decide to do speed sessions, or run a race, you may wish to have a structured warm-up. The following instructions are for you.

Should I stretch?

You don't *have* to stretch. Many people stretch regularly and wouldn't omit

Get your heart beating!

The first part of the warm-up should be devoted to increasing blood flow. To do so requires an increase in your heart rate.

that from their warm-up regime for anything! If you are a stretcher, this would be the time to do it. If you are not used to stretching, it is all right to skip it. There is adequate medical literature to show that there is no difference in the number of running injuries sustained by people who stretch regularly, and people who never stretch. On the other hand, people who 'sometimes' stretch tend to be amongst the most injured group! It may seem surprising, but anecdotal experience would support that as well. Feeling 'tight' is not necessarily improved by stretching. If you over-stretch, you risk injury as well. The response of a muscle which senses itself being over-pulled is to want to contract, to prevent a possible rupture. So, stretch if you like, but stretch sensibly.

TROUBLESHOOTING

Even though I find very little negative to say about running, it wouldn't be fair to think that you will have encountered no hitches on the way to becoming a regular runner. Most of them have very simple remedies.

BLISTERS

The most common causes of blisters in runners are:

– poorly adapted footwear
– excessive friction
– moisture.

The choice of footwear is important in the prevention of injury, and blisters constitute perhaps the mildest of the injuries, yet certainly not the least bothersome. If your running shoes are properly fitted, the risk of blisters is reduced, but you must look further than the fit. Before going for a long run, make sure that there are no pieces of debris inside the shoe. A small piece of straw, or even the tiniest pebble, can create blisters quite quickly. More subtle, an arch support or insole which has slipped, or a loose piece of thread from inner stitching will increase your chances of blistering. You should wear socks. They should be clean and smooth fitting. Wrinkles and binding under the feet or toes should be remedied.

The choice of socks can be very important. To avoid moisture of the feet which can further cause blisters, a sock which 'wicks' the moisture away from the feet can be helpful. Absorbent socks are comfortable (usually natural cotton), but if your feet perspire heavily, the socks will become 'waterlogged' and ineffective in the control of the moisture. In that case the more expensive polypropylene socks will be helpful. Polypropylene wicks away the moisture. Some people find that powder is necessary to keep their feet dry and blister-free. You can also find 'blister-free' socks which are double layered with a thin liner.

Friction, or pressure on the feet, is the final element to keep in mind in avoiding blisters. Walking down the street uses a different footstrike than jogging, or running the same distance. The weight transfer from heel to toe and the force of push-off vary significantly from your walking style. Running positions the foot differently in the shoe, and creates new zones of friction in areas which walking may not have affected. Likewise, running at a faster pace than usual (racing for example), can put pressure on parts of the foot that aren't used to it. This makes blisters likely, especially on a hot day, when your feet may swell in your otherwise roomy training shoes.

To cut down on the amount of friction generated, many strategies can be used. I used to think that the harder I could make the soles of my feet, the less likely I would be to get blisters. I discovered that, totally to the contrary, my hard callouses were unyielding to the movement of the shoe, refusing to conform to my footstrike, and hence, a source of increased blistering!

Having been told that French cyclists would stick a thick piece of steak on their saddle to avoid saddle burn, it occurred to me that the more the soles

of my feet were able to move with my shoes (as would the steak with the cyclists' derrieres) the less likely I would be to have blisters. That indeed, turned out to be the case, and I focus more on keeping my feet moisturised and supple. Further friction-reduction measures include wearing a thin silk inner sock under a sport sock. As long as the inner sock fits snugly and smoothly, it can create a sliding effect between the two layers which seems to absorb the friction between the foot and the insole.

If, despite all this, you find that you blister regularly, it may be that the shoes you have chosen are not suited to your gait. Consider switching models or brands.

When you have a blister
Blisters should be treated appropriately and promptly. Figure 7 shows appropriate treatment of the different stages in blisters.

BRUISED TOENAILS

Sometimes, especially after a long run, you can come back with a sore toenail. It doesn't look bruised, it is just very tender to touch, and a bit red. The nail will then blacken over time, and eventually fall off.

The cause of such injury may be from the foot sliding forward in the shoe, and

Stage	Description	Treatment
1: hot spot	A reddened area, usually located in an area of high friction. It can be quite painful to touch, but the skin has not lifted from the base, nor is there any fluid accumulation.	Avoid any further friction to the area, either by remedying the cause of the irritation, or by adding a protective dressing. Some dressings may actually increase the pressure to the area, if they have insufficient 'give', or if they are too bulky inside a snugly fitted shoe. An ideal dressing would be a product such as 'second skin' which is gelatinous squares which should be cut to roughly the size of the hot spot, then securely taped. They have much the same consistency as skin does, so they absorb the friction well. Be careful to avoid any balling up of the tape under the foot, which can create further irritation.
2: blister	A thin layer of skin has lifted and the resultant pocket is filled with a serous (clear to yellowish) fluid.	• Clean off the skin of the blister thoroughly with a disinfectant such as alcohol. • Sterilise a sharp needle by passing it in a flame until the tip is red hot. • Let the needle cool down without touching it, or letting it touch any surfaces, then, • pierce the skin of the blister in two or three spots at the lowest point. • Gently drain the blister, applying pressure with a gauze pad, or cotton ball, until the fluid is gone. • Apply a dressing, as described above, making sure to leave the skin of the blister intact.
3: blood blisters	As above, except that the pocket may contain blood as well.	As above.

In all cases, keep an eye on the lesion to make sure that there is no redness, increased pain, pus, or other signs of infection in the days following the formation and treatment of the blister. If there is any sign of infection, seek medical attention.

Figure 7: Blisters and their treatment

the nail bumping into the end of the toe box. Improperly fitted or laced shoes may be the culprit. It is sometimes difficult to find just the right balance between lacing up your training shoes tightly enough to prevent sliding forward, but not so tightly as to create discomfort on the top of your foot. So you come home with bruised nails. They can be quite painful, and they throb badly. To relieve the pain, it is recommended by podiatrists and physicians that the pressure under the nail created by the presence of the blood clot be released.

To do so, thoroughly disinfect the nail surface with alcohol. Then, take a paper clip, unbend it, and heat the tip over a flame until it is red hot. Immediately, place the tip of the paper clip on the injured nail. The heat will melt a small opening, through which the blood, and the pressure, should escape to provide you with instant relief. This is not a painful procedure. Disinfect again completely, and dress the nail with a sterile sticking plaster. Monitor for signs of infection and consult a physician immediately if you have concerns.

Proper Toenail Care

Cut your toenails regularly. Cut them straight across the top. Do not cut them in a curve – this can tend to make nails in-grow, and create discomfort in the corners. Do not cut them too short, as they will be uncomfortable when you run.

CHAFING

Once again, friction is the culprit! The more ways you can find to reduce the pressure of clothing against skin, skin against skin, and seams against skin, the more worry-free you will become. The best way to treat chafing is to prevent its occurrence. If you know where it can occur, you can take preventive measures.

Avoid abrasive clothing!

One of the most sensitive areas where chafing occurs is on the chest, above and below the breasts. As the breasts move up and down with the force of gravity, they will pull on the fabric from which your bra is made. Even the best designed, most supportive bra will not be motionless. If the upper or lower hem is poorly finished, stitched with plastic thread, stiff or lacy, you may find that this is a great source of irritation.

The best way to remedy this problem is to turn your bra inside out so the hems face the outside. You can also put sticking plasters on the problem zones, but sometimes they will ball up and create more problems than the hems. Smaller breasted women may choose not to wear bras, but they may still find (as do many male runners) that their nipples will chafe as they rub against the outer clothing (t-shirt or jersey). Sticking plasters across the sensitive zone are

usually quite effective.

Other zones of chafing where you should look at clothing construction as a possible cause or solution would include:

- The crotch of tights or bike pants. They should have a built-in gusset, and not a centre seam.
- The armholes of form-fitting sports tops. They should allow total freedom of movement.
- The leg holes of panties. Make sure they are not too tight.

Watch out for skin!

Skin against skin can cause problems for runners of all shapes and sizes. I, for example, have very narrow hips and as a result, the top of my thighs chafe as they rub together. Much heavier built runners may not have the same problem. The under-arm is another area which chafes readily. It is often recommended that you avoid this kind of chafing by applying a barrier ointment (Vaseline, or a similar oil-based ointment) or talcum powder. The rationale is that the barrier will rub, and not the skin. Or, in my case, wear smooth fitting short lycra tights to reduce the skin to skin contact.

There is no long-term, or even medium-term problem associated with chafing. In most cases, by the next day the irritation will be much improved, and by the end of the week, forgotten.

RUNNER'S DIARRHOEA – THE 'RUNS'

Running seems to increase the motility of the bowel. This is especially true before racing (nerves) and in stressful situations. Dehydration, bouncing, redistribution of the blood supply to the exercising muscles are all reasons to explain why runners often get 'the runs' while training or racing. You may also find as you get fitter that you have bowel movements more frequently, even outside of the running sessions.

If diarrhoea is a problem, there are a few approaches you can take. First of all, do your best to have a bowel movement prior to your run. Secondly, play around with your food intake. It may be that you will find that some foods are more likely to cause problems than others. Coffee, spices and alcohol are all contributors to increased bowel motility, and should be avoided. Lactose intolerance may also be an important factor in 'the runs', and avoiding milk and dairy products may help you as well. Proper hydration is important, so make sure you drink adequate amounts of fluids during the day.

Record your approach to this problem in your training log, as well as the outcome of the strategy, and see what works best for you.

RUNNER'S STITCH

Especially among beginning runners, a 'stitch' in the side is a common occurrence. It doesn't sound like much, but can actually be quite a debilitating problem. You have just started running, and you feel pretty good, but all of a sudden, there is a niggling sensation under the rib cage on the right side. Ow! It feels progressively worse, and sometimes moves to the shoulder. It can feel pretty dreadful!

It is thought that the cause of the stitch may be related to the diaphragm, but there are many other factors which may contribute. You can stop running. The pain usually stops as well. If it doesn't, the cause of the pain may not be a stitch, and you should contact your doctor. You can also try to 'run through' the pain, meaning ignoring it for a few minutes and running until the pain disappears. That is not a very satisfactory solution, however, as it doesn't feel good, and because it is always a better idea to respect strong messages such as this.

Some people find that taking deep breaths, and particularly exhaling force-fully, can help to relieve stitch pain. Other solutions include applying deep pressure with your fingers to the area where the stitch is occurring, or walking for a little while. Sometimes the stitch can be bad enough that there is some residual soreness for a few days following the episode. Inadequate abdominal musculature may be responsible, in some cases, for the stitch. My experience would confirm this, as I have only ever suffered from stitches in the early months following the birth of my children, when my abdominal musculature was certainly well below its usual strength. Some tummy strengthening exercise can help. I have also experienced more stitches when running fast, and when running downhill. Remember that stitches plague mainly beginning runners, and with time and practice, will become less of a problem for you.

SHORT WINDEDNESS

If you get terribly out of breath with what seems to be moderate exercise, a number of things may be not quite right. You may be training too fast. You can't skip steps. Take your time and make sure you have allowed yourself to arrive at an appropriate level of fitness in a progressive way. Are you running in a group? It is easy to try to follow the rhythm of the group rather than that of your body, and if you are feeling particularly winded, it may be that ability levels are different. Don't measure yourself against the others in the group. A heavier, apparently less fit friend may have a special aptitude for running, and your feeling winded may reflect the fact that you are moving on too quickly by trying to keep up with her.

If you have problems with short windedness, check your pulse rate. Where does it fit in the target exercise heart rate table (Figure 4)? If it is in the high end of the target zone, or above, definitely slow down your pace. If, after toning down your training, you still don't feel right, consult your doctor and report the problem, as well as the adjustments you have made. Some investigation, or simply reassurance, may be in order.

SORE LEGS

We'll talk about full-blown injuries further on in the book. For right now, we want to discuss the kinds of soreness a beginning runner might have. This isn't an injury, but it is nonetheless a problem to be dealt with. Let's face it: if you are starting to run after years of inactivity, your legs will have some waking up to do. They will be tired in the beginning, and instead of just being attached to your body, will let you know that they are there. It is usually not a bad feeling all in all. Sometimes though, the feeling is more than just an increased awareness. Your legs may be very stiff. Often beginning runners will complain about soreness in the middle, or lower part of their calf muscles on both sides.

It feels like they have been tightened up like a rubber band ready to spring. The first step out of bed, or up from a seated position, when you haven't been walking in a while, can sometimes be very surprising. What to do?

Hopefully, if you have done your running in a progressive enough manner, this won't happen to you very often. But, once in a while, it will, thanks to a longer than usual run, or a very hilly course. The first step is to take things easy until the legs come back to normal. You may take a day or two off, until your legs feel all right again. Walking instead of running may be of some benefit. Secondly, try to identify what factors may have caused the stiffness in the first place, and avoid causing it again. Thirdly, make sure that the stiffness you feel is just stiffness. If it doesn't go away after taking the suggested measures, if it is unilateral (affecting one leg only), or if it is getting worse rather than better, seek medical attention.

'Shin splints' are a common cause of leg pain in beginning runners. In my high school days, runners could be seen at the side of the track, holding paper cups filled with water which had been frozen. The top half of the cup was torn away, and the new runners would be massaging their painful legs with this conveniently shaped ice cube in its paper cup holder. Although the absolute cause of shin splints is not clear, many contributing factors are:

– running too much, too soon: the bones become stronger with weight-bearing exercise, but need time to become mature and healthy. Bone fitness takes some time, and certainly more than does cardio-vascular and muscular fitness.

– not wearing the correct shoes. Heavy pronators who are not wearing stable enough shoes, or runners with a bit of extra weight who do not have sufficiently cushioned shoes, may have more problems with shin splints.

– running on hard surfaces: although soft surfaces have their disadvantages too, because they do not enhance foot stability, the jarring effect of hard surfaces can contribute to shin splints. Alternating runs on grass or even beaches with road runs, or making sure that all runs contain some soft surfaces, is desirable.

– not recognising (or not paying heed to) early warning signs of overdoing, and not moderating your activity soon enough.

CHAPTER THREE

Moving On –
No Longer a Beginner

After four to six months of regular running, you have gone well beyond the beginner stage. Running is a part of your life, and you no longer have to make a great effort to fit it into your activities. It is a natural part of your day. You probably don't run alone any more, or at least some days you have company. Perhaps one day, you bumped into an acquaintance while you were out running; 'Oh, I didn't know you ran too!', and before long, you made dates to run together, or at least to share part of a run.

If you haven't met any runners yet, try to go out of your way to meet some. There are lots of ways to do that. You can go to the local running-shoe store, and ask if they can tell you about groups which might be of your ability level. They can also tell you about local clubs. In some areas, clubs are the lifeblood of running circles. They may be competitive in nature, but they are likely to have a jogging group for recreational

runners as well. In other areas, clubs may be purely social. Try the Internet for information about clubs in your area. Contact the British Athletics Association, or visit their 'club-finder' website (www.british-athletics.co.uk/clubs). I met my husband in my running club, but the number of other good friends I have made just by approaching a runner who was going my pace and saying 'mind if I join you?' is amazing! Your running will be enriched by contact with other runners who are motivated like you to find a good balance of

---

Julie W.

I started running when I separated from my husband. I had always wanted to run, but didn't have the courage to. But once I stepped out of that relationship, I had to start doing things for myself. I had been timid about making the initial start, like joining a club and meeting people. However, even just jogging made me feel good inside. It improved my self-esteem.

---

physical well-being. Keep reading running magazines. Read about training techniques, and about the experiences of the champions, and of Jane and John Doe, ordinary runners.

If you wish to take your running one step further, you will now need to individualise your training. The basic principles of training will not change, but the goals and the manner in which they are implemented will.

DESIGN YOUR OWN TRAINING PROGRAMME

Even without a coach, you can plan a programme which will meet your needs. Start by re-reading the **Golden Rules of Running**, because they are just as important now as they were when you started. Your attitude towards running may have changed somewhat since you started. You are probably more focused. Whereas you may have felt dubious about running in the beginning, you may now feel very committed. You may be quite relaxed about your running, or

you may be quite intense, but no matter what your approach, you will be most likely to succeed with a flexible programme. This is why you need to have a programme which is suited to your personality, as well as to your physical needs.

If you are secretly hoping that starting a running programme will make you look like Cindy Crawford, and that you will automatically (or even progressively!) turn into a drop dead gorgeous string bean, please re-evaluate. Take a look at your parents. How are they built? Did you inherit the right genes to look that way? Running will help you to look better and feel better, but changing body morphology is not the kind of goal that will help you maintain a training programme.

DEFINE YOUR GOALS

As when you first started running, it is good to keep a goal in mind. It will keep you focused. Perhaps you would like to run a 10 kilometre race in your

---

THE GOLDEN RULES OF RUNNING (A Reminder)

1. The body is still the boss, so listen to its messages (fatigue, pain, strain).
2. Rest is an integral part of training, and must be included in any sensible plan.
3. Being fit means finding the optimal level at which your body can function. It does not mean pushing your body over the edge by excessive physical activity.

---

city, or in the town where you are planning on holidaying next June. Whatever the goal, write it in your training log as a reminder, and as the basis for your training plans.

BE CONSISTENT

It is much better to run a little bit every day than to run heaps once a week. You can't put a week's worth of training into a day, no matter how hard you try. It doesn't have the same effect. Furthermore, the more regularly you train, the easier it is to follow through on your goals. It is easier to organise your life. So, run consistently, and regularly.

PERIODISE!

Periodisation is the technical term used to describe cycles of work and rest within a training programme. As when we discussed lifting a heavy rock, the purpose of periodisation is to lead you to a better level of fitness by gradually increasing the workload, and balancing it with rest. Periodisation is also about alternating hard and easy, long and short, and fast and slow. An important part of periodisation is recognising that increases are not always necessary. Sometimes decreases will produce rebound improvement that could never be achieved by continuously elevating the amount and intensity of exercise.

How do you use periodisation?

Every week, every month, and even every year, periodisation should be incorporated into your training plan. Each week will comprise a variety of work-outs, from gentle, slow recovery runs, to harder speed-oriented training (I'll describe some of them later). The variety prepares you in many different ways: it trains your mind, your heart, your muscles and keeps you from going 'stale'. Each week, you will use the concept of periodisation to enhance recovery. If one day's run is more difficult, either due to the length or the speed of the run, the next day should be more gentle. Using the hard/easy pattern, you will periodise your week, and improve your running.

Periodising over a month

If you are currently running three times a week, but would like to move forward, you might do the following:

week 1: run 2 x 30 mins + 1 x 45 mins
total running time: 105 mins

week 2: run 2 x 40 mins + 1 x 50 mins
total running time: 130 mins

week 3: run 3 x 30 mins + 1 x 55 mins
total running time: 145 mins

week 4: run 2 x 30 mins + 1 x 45 mins
total running time: 105 mins

This example shows increasing mileage

over a three week period, but a fourth week allows recovery. What if you don't feel as if you need recovery? Take it anyway! You will have to pay for it, otherwise, further down the road. That rest week is a great time to let yourself be flexible: run when you feel like it, skip a run, or do something else you may have wanted to do for a long time.

ADAPT YOUR PLAN TO YOUR LIFESTYLE

Some days, you'll have to miss a run. Your child might be sick, you might be sick yourself, you might have twisted your ankle, or there might be a hurricane raging. Your training prog-ramme must be flexible enough to adapt to such unplanned events. It must take into consideration your personal lifestyle. Okay, we agree that less than three runs a week will not give you optimum benefit, but life is full of unexpected events, so there will always be unplanned rest days. Take it all in your stride, write off those days, and look forward to when you will next get some time for running.

VARY YOUR TRAINING

Not only will bringing some variety into your training improve your physical condition, it will also leave you fresh and light, not flat from monotonous training. You can vary the kind of training you do, as well as the training sites. Run on the beach one day, on the roads the next, on the hills the next, and then on the track. This way, you will protect your legs and avoid boredom.

Once you have built a solid base of slow, easy running, you may wish to improve your speed or your endurance. In this section, we will discuss some of the many options which are available. If you find a particular work-out which appeals to you, that does not mean that is the only one you should do. You risk getting stuck in a physical and mental rut if you do that. Change around from week to week, focusing on different aspects of your training at a time. In this way you can develop your full potential as a runner.

DIFFERENT TYPES OF TRAINING

Run – When I refer to a 'run', I am talking about a work-out during which your heart rate is in the middle of the target zone described in Figure 4. This is a run where you are relaxed, and barely 'working'. This may also be referred to as a 'recovery run', when it is compared to the more intense work-outs.

Long run – The only difference between this and the first category is the duration of the run. A 'long run' would be the

equivalent of the weekend outings we have discussed in the beginner's programme. The duration can be as much as, or even slightly more than, double the regular run. One long run every week, or every two weeks (if more than two times the regular distance) is recommended.

Fartlek – This term comes from the Swedish word, which means 'speed play'. Fartlek refers to a kind of work-out which uses sporadic accelerations with no particular structure. The runner is perfectly free to decide when and for how long she will pick up the pace. Examples of fartlek exercises might be:

– 35 minute run with spurts on the up hills

– 35 minute run, with a speed burst between every fourth telephone pole, for 10–15 minutes of the run

– a self-designed spontaneous mixture of speed bursts according to how you feel.

Intervals – This is a more structured kind of work-out than fartlek. In interval training, you run a given distance at a given speed, and then, after a given rest, you repeat the distance a given number of times. The speed, the rest period, and the distance will depend on your goals and your ability level. Typical interval work-outs might be:

12 x 200m, 100m jog recovery, or
5 x 1000m, 3 mins jog recovery

Work-out	Explanation	Pace	Purpose
12 x 200 metres – recovery 100 metres jog	recovery time equal to exertion time	steady	conditioning
12 x 200 metres – recovery 200 metres jog	recovery time equal to 1.5–2 times exertion time	moderate	conditioning/tempo
8 x 200 metres – recovery 2–3 minutes walk	recovery time far greater than exertion time = complete recovery	very quick	conditioning/pace tolerance
20 x 200 metres – 30 seconds recovery	recovery time less than exertion time	steady	conditioning for advanced runner – improvement of recoverability

Figure 8: Variations of the work-out

6 x 3 mins at race pace, 2 mins jog recovery

All these 'givens' are important to making the work-out achieve the desired purpose. We will take the example of the 12 x 200 metres with 100 metres jog recovery to illustrate this point. Look at Figure 8 to understand the physiological impact that changing the rest interval, or the load, has on the work-out.

This table demonstrates the specificity of the various work-outs. Any one of these work-outs may be appropriate for you at a given time. They are not, however, interchangeable, as suggested by the heading **purpose**.

15/15 or 30/30 – This is an excellent base-building work-out which requires a stopwatch or a second hand. You run for 15 seconds at a fast clip, and then walk for the same amount of time. Do 5 to 10 minutes of 15/15 (or 30/30), and repeat one to two times after a brief

---

A guide to adding quality work

- Set an adequate base of slow, easy running, before adding in quality work.

- Be consistentent: try to run as regularly as you can, throughout the week/month/year.

- Alternate hard/easy work.

- Vary your work-outs (see Figure 8).

---

jogged recovery. A further variant of this work-out would be to run one to two minutes fast followed by one to two minutes slowly. A slow running recovery replaces the walk.

Hill training – hills can be used for training in many ways. Just going for a run on the hills can turn a regular run into a challenging cardio-vascular and neuro-muscular exercise. You can also use hill work to increase strength by bounding up a short hill with exaggerated use of the arms, and a high knee lift.

How should I choose what to do?

As always, it is your choice. Your schedule, your strength and weaknesses, will guide you. In the absence of a personal coach to help you make such decisions, Figure 9 suggests how many of which types of work-outs you should do, based on your total work-outs per week. The more times you run, the more opportunities there are for diversifying! Even if you are not planning on racing, or competitive running, you may wish to improve your fitness, and enjoy your running further, by adding one more intense run. You should alternate your hard and easy running to respect the principles of periodisation.

Remember, quality work should not be done prior to establishing a solid base of slow constant running, nor can it replace the base work. It is an adjunct to your regular running programme.

WRITING A TRAINING PROGRAMME

Sample programmes

Some sample training programmes are featured here, not so that you can rush out and try to follow them, but rather to show you how you can make these different kinds of work-outs fit into a week, a month, or a season of running. I have included the programme of a four day-a-week fitness runner, a four day-a-week competitive runner, and a serious seven to ten times a week highly competitive runner. Please note the way the mileage varies from week to week as well as how there is alternation between high and low intensity, and long and short runs.

Muriel H.

I started running when I was 46. I had always been a hiker and a walker. I pushed my husband into it years before, thinking it would be good for him. And he'd try to get me out but it just wasn't my time yet. And then all of a sudden, it was my time. I just put on my shoes, and went out!

It wasn't bad to start with as I was generally quite fit. I did 15 minutes the first time and went a wee bit faster the next. Then I went a bit further.

Now I've run a half marathon!

Your own training programme

You have seen the way running programmes are set up, and you have been given the rules as to what you should avoid (too much, too soon), and what you should keep in mind (goal setting, progressive build-up, adequate rest). Let's try to tailor a plan which will suit your individual needs. A programme should not cover more than about three months of running at a time. This does not mean that you should not have longer term goals. It is just impractical to try to plan the specifics too far in advance. Use the following work-sheet to write your programme. If you can, share it with a qualified coach, exercise physiologist, or experienced runner for their feed-back. Most importantly, keep an open mind to the messages your body sends you. Be willing to adapt your plan as you go on, if you find that anything doesn't click.

The Non-Competitive Runner

The Three-Month Planner

1. Using Figure 12, plot your current total weekly running time on the planner against Week One.
2. Identify your weekly running time goal (it should probably not exceed your current time by more than 35% – see Figure 14).
3. Set a target date for achieving that

goal (approximately three months is recommended).

4. Count the weeks and plot the goal on the appropriate line of the planner.

5. Plot your 'rest' weeks. The week following your target will be a rest week. Counting backwards from that week, earmark every fourth week as a 'rest' week, and accordingly plot slightly less than your current weekly running time for those.

6. Draw a light pencil line to connect this week's (current) running time with your running time goal.

7. Fill in evenly spaced steps in the cycles between each rest week to loosely follow the pencil line.

8. Look at your work schedule, family plans and make any changes that are necessary (i.e.; move a rest week to avoid a clash with a heavy working week, or extend the last cycle to allow you to achieve your target running time while you're on holiday, etc.).

Remember that high mileage is followed by low mileage, as high intensity should be followed by low intensity. Each week you can look at your total running time and break it down into an appropriate number and variety of runs. If you like to be well-organised you can plot these weeks in advance as well.

Week	# Runs	Variations	Total running time (mins)
1	4	easy runs only	200–220
2	4	• 1 x 60 min long run	200–220
3	4	• one run on more challenging terrain (hills/beach/etc.)	200–220
4	4	• 1 x 70 min long run	220–250
5	3	easy runs only – take a break this week!	180–200
6	4	• 1 x 70–80 min long run	220–250
7	4	• one run on challenging terrain	220–250
8	4	• 1 x 80 min long run	240–260
9	4	• one run faster than usual run • one run on challenging terrain	240–260
10	3	take it easy!	200–220
11	4	• one run on challenging terrain • 1 x 80 min long run	240–260
12	4	• one faster than usual run • 1 x 85 min long run	250–270

Figure 9: Sample training programme for a four-day-a-week non-competitive runner

Week	# Runs	Variations	Total running time (mins)
1	4	• 2 x 5 min (15/15) 2 min* *5 min between sets* • long run – 60 min	200–220
2	4	• 10 min fartlek • 1 x long run – 70 min	240–260
3	4 to 5	• 10 x 200 m (on the track) * *45 seconds* • 5 min sustained run • 1 x long run – 70 min	280–300
4	3	easy runs only	180–200
5	4	• 1 x 10 min (15/15) • 1 x long run – 60 min	240–260
6	5	• 8 hill spurts (approx 60 metres) • 1 x long run – 70–75 min	280–300
7	4 to 5	• 7 x 400 m * *2 min jog* • hill run (regular run on hilly terrain) 1 x long run 75–80 min	320–340
8	3	easy runs only	180–220
9	4	• 12 min fartlek • 1 x long run 60–70 min	280–300
10	4	• 10 x (1 min fast/1 min slow) • 1 x long run – 75 min	320–340
11	4 to 5	• 12 x 200 m * *45 secs* • 2 x 5 min sustained runs,* *5 min* • 1 x long run 75–80 min	360–380
12	3	easy runs only, or race, if desired	180–220

* *recovery time between efforts*

Figure 10: Sample training programme for a four-day-a-week competitive runner

The Weekly Planner

1. Look the week over and decide how you would like to spread the total running time (e.g.; long run on Sunday, short run on Friday, rest on Wednesday). Create your own graph, following the example of Figure 13 'Weekly Planner'. Remember to take your work and family life into consideration when plotting daily running times.

2. Shade each entry according to what

Week	# Runs	Variations	Total running time (mins)
1	7	• 30/30 x 15 mins • 10–15 min tempo run	320–340
2	7	• 20 x 200 m * *30 secs* • 10–15 min tempo run • 1 x long run – 80 min	360–380
3	7	• 3 x 2000 m * *5 min* • 15–20 min tempo run • 1 x long run – 90 min	400–420
4	6	• fartlek, or striders • 10–15 min tempo run or race	320–340
5	7	• 20 x 200 m * *30 secs* • 5 x 1000 m * *3 min* • 1 x long run – 80 min	360–380
6	7	• 15 x 400 m * *110m jog* • 3 x 2000 m * *5 min* • 1 x long run – 80–90 min	400–420
7	8	• fartlek • 3 x 10 min tempo runs • 1 x long run – 90 + min	440–460
8	6	• striders or fartlek • 1 x 5–10 km race	320–340
9	7	• 10 x 400m * *200m jog* • 4 x 1000m * *4 min* • 1 x 80 min long run	440–460
10	7	• 6 x 500 m * *2½ min* • 1 x race – 5000 m • 1 x easy long run	400–420
11	8	• 10 x 200m * *200m slow jog* • 4 x 800 m * *3½ min* • 2 x 10 min tempo runs	360–380
12	6	• 3 x 1 mile * *5–6 min* • race – 10 000 m • 1 x slow recovery run	320–340

* *recovery time between efforts*
note the 'sharpening' nature of both the total running time and the quality loads.

Figure 11: Sample training programme for a seven-day-a-week competitive runner

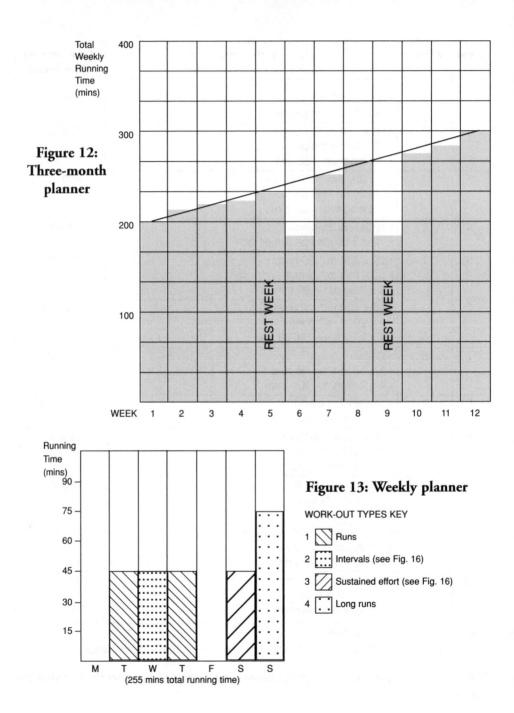

Total Weekly Running Time (mins)

Figure 12: Three-month planner

REST WEEK

REST WEEK

WEEK 1 2 3 4 5 6 7 8 9 10 11 12

Running Time (mins)

Figure 13: Weekly planner

WORK-OUT TYPES KEY

1 [N] Runs

2 [:::] Intervals (see Fig. 16)

3 [//] Sustained effort (see Fig. 16)

4 [: .] Long runs

M T W T F S S
(255 mins total running time)

There is no absolute rule as to how much you can or should increase your running time over a *three month* training programme. The following table provides suggestions for possible target weekly running time increases:

Current maximum running time	Target maximum running time
100–150 mins	150–225 mins
150–200 mins	225–300 mins
200–250 mins	260–375 mins
250–300 mins	300–420 mins
300–350 mins	360–490 mins
350–400 mins	420–560 mins
400–450 mins	460–585 mins

Figure 14: How much should I increase my weekly running time?

type of work-out you plan for that day. Use Figure 15 'Number of Work-outs per Week' as a guide.
3. Choose individual work-outs from Figure 19 'Quality Work-outs' or from variations or inventions of your own which fit the bill.

If you like, you can transfer all this information to a format such as Figure 17 'The Training Programme Planner' which shows you your three-month plan at a glance.

Figure 16 reviews the main training work-out types that you may be interested in using. All possible work-outs are not covered, particularly the very high intensity work-outs which are used to help an athlete 'peak' for major competitions. I suggest consulting Jon Ackland and Brett Reid's *The Power to Perform* for those.

What to do when the programme is finished

You can always repeat the process. By this time, you will have a better understanding of your ability, and what goals

# runs /week	Work-out types			
	1	2	3	4
3–4	1	choose 1 x type 2 *or* type 3 work-out*		1
5	2	choose 1 x type 2 & 1 x type 3 work-out		1
6	3	1	1	1
7 or more	3	1	2	1

*I would suggest alternating from week to week

Figure 15: Number of work-outs per week

Group	Work-out	Description	Pace	Goals
1	runs	regular training runs	a	• basic aerobic conditioning
2	intervals	segmented exercises where you run for 15 seconds to 3 minutes, with recovery equal to or less than running time	c	• working above threshold for brief intervals in order to improve the body's ability to train aerobically, below threshold
3	sustained effort (referred to as 'tempo running', or 'time trials')	this can either be segmented (more than one repetition of a harder piece lasting anywhere from 3 to 10 minutes, or more, with recovery less than running time), or can be simply one long piece or a race	b	• work at threshold for a sustained period of time in order to improve the pace at which threshold is reached
4	long runs	125–200% of regular daily training distance	a	• increase aerobic capacity by increasing capillarisation, and utilisation of efficient energy sources • when preparing for longer races, accustom the body to the biomechanical effects of prolonged exercise

A reminder: The threshold is the point at which we are no longer able to maintain aerobic steady-state exercise

Training pace: a – Talking pace.

  b – It would be rather hard to talk at this pace, but it is not so hard that you cannot finish the prescribed distance at the pace you started with.

  c – Intense. Make sure you can do the prescribed number of repetitions at the chosen pace, but you should have no energy to spare!

Figure 16: Work-out rationale and explanation

Week	# Runs	Work-outs	Total running time (mins)
1		• • •	
2		• • •	
3		• • •	
4		• • •	
5		• • •	
6		• • •	
7		• • •	
8		• • •	
9		• • •	
10		• • •	
11		• • •	
12		• • •	

Transcribe the plan into a format you can follow, and off you go!

Figure 17: Training programme planner

USING A TRAINING PROGRAMME

- A training programme can be used as a guide, a reminder of your goals and plans.

- A training programme is not a recipe written in stone. It should be a dynamic plan which can adapt to your changing needs.

- The body remains the boss. Learning to listen to its messages, and adapting the programme accordingly is the secret to success.

are realistic for you. You may be able (and want!) to go yet further than on the last programme. Do not go straight into the new programme however. Give yourself a slightly longer 'rest' period (i.e.: take two or three weeks of light mileage), and then start a second programme. You should start not where you left off, nor where you initially started, but right in the middle, at the second cycle. You can also consider progressing to a competitive training programme, the details of which follow.

It is very important not to increase your training too quickly. Even though you may feel very fit from the cardio-vascular and muscular standpoint, you must make sure that your bones, too, are ready to take the increased pounding. We have all been told repeatedly that weight bearing is good for our bone density. It is, however, important to understand that our bones do not get stronger immediately. When you start, or significantly increase, a training programme, your bones may go through a phase of increased

fragility, prior to growing stronger. This is why shin splints and even stress fractures can occur in beginning (or over-ambitious) runners.[5] Women seem to be particularly susceptible to these types of injuries, with as much as twelve times as many stress fractures as men, according to some studies. One reason for that is thought to be the cessation of menstruation noted in some endurance athletes. We will devote an entire chapter to that subject further on.

My personal experience on the subject of bone fragility and increased training is a perfect example of why caution must be taken. I have been running for 23 years. During that period, I had virtually never been injured. As a teenager, I 'overdid' it occasionally, and incurred one or two problems at that time. As an adult, I have almost never had to take off more than a few days, to rest

---

5 For more information on this phenomenon, which has been labelled 'osteoclonal excavation', please refer to the brilliant book by Tim Noakes, entitled *Love of Running* (Leisure Press, Champaign, IL, 1991).

sore muscles or joints. I attributed that to a very rational and prudent approach to my running. I truly don't run when I don't feel right. I like to feel good when I run, because I run for enjoyment.

Between 1987 and 1993, I had to put my running on the back-burner. I was working full-time night shift, had young children, and couldn't devote enough energy to competitive running. I trained regularly, but raced rarely, and accumulated a modest number of miles each week. My fortunes changed when my husband finished his studies, and once again, I had time to train seriously. Within six months, my competitive performances were back to what they had been when I was 23

years old, and my running felt great! As described above, my cardio-vascular and muscular fitness was excellent. Unaware, at that time, of the phenomenon of increased weakness of bones during augmented training, I also had my first stress fracture, which curtailed my activities for months! Don't let this happen to you.

Once upon a time there was a woman named Anne. She was very interested in becoming fit and healthy. Although she had not practised any sport since the age of 15, she decided to run, in order to firm her buttocks, and perhaps, to distinguish herself in competitive events. She soon found that running was indeed to her liking, and every day, shod in marvellous shoes, with soles of air, she bounced over the countryside, devoured the pavement, feeling lighter each day. Pleased with the apparent ease with which she had become an efficient runner, she ran further and faster. She never rested, never took a day off. 'More! More!' she thought to herself. One day, she awoke with some soreness in her lower leg. She would not be deterred. She ran as usual, but felt tired and less responsive. The next day, the pain was again present, and once again she kept driving on, ever forward! After a week of discomfort, Anne finally consulted a physician to determine the cause of her ails. After lengthy conferences, the verdict was uttered: stress fracture! Anne was to stop running for four to six weeks.

Do you remember the tale of the tortoise and the hare?

TRAINING TO RACE

Many fitness runners enjoy racing. It is yet another opportunity to commune with interesting people who share your passion. It also provides an opportunity to measure yourself: to see if you are indeed running faster, and more strongly than before. I would encourage you to enter a race after you've been running for six months or so.

Keep an eye on the local paper, or check out the local sports store to see when a race might be held in your area. If you can, choose to run a large, rather than a small race, so that you can bury

yourself in the masses. Don't start with a marathon right off the bat, but rather, try a shorter 10km race, and work yourself up to longer distance events. Once you have decided what event you would like to focus on, you can design a programme that will allow you to come to the starting line well prepared.

The competitive runner's training programme

This programme is designed to help you to get ready for your first race. It will not be the same as one designed for an elite runner and experienced racer who would want to peak for an event. Peaking is the art of reaching absolute optimum fitness and having it fine-tuned for the needed event. It involves incorporating carefully designed work-outs at crucial points in your build-up to a race. It also entails the use of secondary competitions (less important ones) and rest in the final days or weeks prior to the main event. This programme isn't designed to help you peak for an event, but rather, to build a base of aerobic fitness which is enhanced by well-chosen quality work. The base building and sharpening programme we are outlining should allow you to make the transition from running for fitness to running for performance. If you have not already trained to a non-competitive runner's

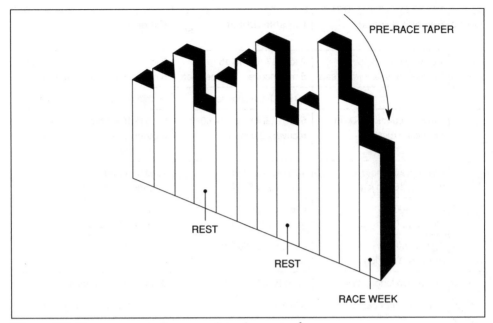

PRE-RACE TAPER

REST

REST

RACE WEEK

Figure 18: Race preparation running time graph

programme, read through the instructions above, then:

1. Plot your highest quantity week to fall three weeks prior to the race.

2. Make sure that the race falls on a rest week, and that the week preceding race week is a relatively low 'total-time-running' week (see Figure 18).

3. Incorporate work-outs from both type 1 and type 2 groups. In the bigger weeks, increase the number of repetitions, or the duration of the work-outs. In smaller weeks, and particularly in race week, reduce the number of repetitions, or the duration.

4. Have 2–4 days between the last quality work-out and the final race.

5. Transcribe your plan to the suitable format, and have fun going for it!

RUNNING YOUR FIRST RACE

Choosing the race

The best way to choose a race is to find an event which takes place at a convenient time in the year (in the middle of a holiday, at the end of a light period at work, on a long weekend when

Group	Beginning runner	Capable runner	Expert runner
2	1 to 3 x 5 min 15/15 5 min recovery between sets	2 to 3 x 7 min 15/15 5 min recovery between sets	2 to 3 x 8 12 min 15/15 or 30/30 5 min recovery between sets
	5 to 10 min short fartlek	10 to 20 min short fartlek	30 min or more of short fartlek
	4 to 8 hill bursts 50–60 m recovery 2 min jog	5 to 10 hill bursts 50–60 m recovery 2 min jog	2 x 5 to 10 hill bursts 50–60 m recovery 2 min between sprints 10 min between sets
	8 to 10 x 200 m recovery 100 m jog	10 to 15 x 200 m recovery 100 m jog	15 to 30 x 200 m recovery 30 seconds
	4 to 6 x 400 m recovery 200 m jog	6 to 10 x 400 m recovery 200 m jog	12 to 20 x 400 m recovery 100–200 m jog, or 45 sec
	3 x 600–800 m recovery 3 min jog	3 to 5 x 600–800 m recovery 3–4 min jog	5 to 10 x 600–800 m recovery 2–3 min jog
3	5 to 10 min long fartlek	10 to 20 min long fartlek	30 to 45 min long fartlek
	5 kms on hilly course	5 to 8 kms on the hills	10 kms or more on hilly course
	3 x 2 to 4 min sustained run	3 x 5 to 7 min sustained run	3 x 10 min 2 x 15 min 1 x 20 min or more sustained run
	3 x 1000 m recovery = running time	4 to 6 x 1000 m recovery = running time	up to 10 x 1000 m recovery 2:30 to 3 min
		2 to 3 x 2000 m recovery 4 to 5 min jog	3 to 5 x 2000 m recovery 3:30 to 4:30 min
			3 x 3000 m recovery 5 min
			1000 m/2000 m/3000 m/5000 m recovery 3:30 to 6 mins
		races 3 kms to 10 kms	races 3 kms to 20 kms
4	45 to 60 min	60 to 160 min (12 to 25 kms)	20 to 35 kms

Figure 19: Quality work-outs by group

you know you'll be free), which is convenient to your home or holiday spot, and which is a suitable distance. A good first race distance is 10 kms. Ten kilometres (or 6.2 miles) is long enough to make you feel a great sense of accomplishment, but not so long that it requires extensive preparation. Once again, the local running clubs, specialised sporting goods stores, municipal or university athletic departments should be able to help you find the appropriate event. For your first race, start making plans about three months ahead of time. Set out your training schedule, to get physically prepared.

Now you need to run it! Find out what time the race is to take place, and get there early enough to pick up your race number, warm up a little bit, and figure out what the course will be. If you can, pick up your race number the night before. Keep some safety pins in your sport bag so that you can pin on the number, in case pins are not provided at the start. Pin the race number on the front of your race jersey.

At the number pick-up, there will probably be a map of the race route. Take a look at it so you know where you are going to be headed. There will probably be water stops on the route, and on a hot day, it is particularly helpful to know ahead of time where water will be available.

Put on clean running socks. Make sure there are no stones, thorns, wrinkles, or loose threads in your shoes. You don't want to get blisters. If it is to be a long race, and if you tend to chafe at the top of your thighs, or under your arms, rub some Vaseline in those areas.

For competitive runners

More dynamic work is in order for warming up for a race, or a speed session. On the road, track, or a flat piece of grass, you should choose a 50 metre segment, and skip bouncily from one end to the other. Come back to the start, and do another length, but this time, don't skip. Do 'high knees'. High knees means running on your toes and concentrating on raising your knees as high as you can, without any back extension (your feet stay in front of your body). Then do 'butt kicks', which are the opposite. With your knees pointing almost straight down, focus on the back part of your stride, with your heels almost touching your backside. You can also run 2 to 3 'stride-outs'. A stride-out is a short run where you increase your speed progressively over the distance to attain a full stride and a fast pace by the end. The intensity of the stride-out depends on the distance of the race, or the speed session you are going to undertake. Your speed at the end of the stride-out should be just slightly faster than the speed you plan to achieve in your race, or your session. Once you have completed your stride-outs, you are ready to take off your warm-up suit, and go to the line.

Butterflies

All runners get butterflies when they line up to race. The good thing is that most runners learn how to use them to enhance their performance. The rush of adrenalin associated with pre-race jitters can push you faster than you might think possible. Just remember:

• everyone else has them

• they'll fly away with the starter's gun

• they'll help you run fast

• they'll be the first thing you forget after you finish the race!

For a long race, very little warm-up will be necessary. If it is very cold out, it will be important to jog about until you feel nice and warm. Then do your regular stretching routine, and very slowly jog around until it is almost time to go. Don't take off your warm-up suit, or outer clothes, until the last minute before you get to the line. If there are scads of people, and you are not sure you will be able to keep your warm-up clothes from getting picked up by someone else, you can get a big plastic rubbish bag, and cut a hole for your head. It will keep you warm, and you can discard it when the gun goes

off. Not everyone can stand right on the starting line, and as this is your first race, you can stay well back of the front line to wait for the gun to be fired. Front runners will go off like a shot, and may drag you along at a speed which is faster than you should go. Furthermore, it is all too easy to fall, when fast runners are pushing from the back to get up to their rightful places.

When the gun goes off, start your stopwatch, and start running gently. Hold yourself back. The classic mistake is to go out too fast, and then to burn out at the end of the race. It is amazing how the excitement of the group will pull you along when you don't intend to go so fast. Furthermore, you will be nervous yourself, and the influx of adrenalin will push you faster than you mean to go. The key to success is pacing yourself so that you finish as fast as you started. The big surprise for most beginners is to discover that times which may have felt exceptionally fast in training seem much easier in a race.

Should I eat or drink during a race?

In a race shorter than 5kms, you will probably not need to eat or drink. In longer distance events, that will depend on the weather conditions. When it is hot, it is imperative to drink water, or electrolyte-replacement drinks, every fifteen minutes or so. You can stop

Object	Comments
running shoes	• one pair for the warm-up • one pair for the race if you have 2 pairs (make sure they are clean and dry, with no loose threads, or seams which might cause blisters) • change back to warm-up shoes after the race
three running tops	• one for the warm-up • one for the race (long sleeves if it is cold) • one dry one for after the race (important, it is easy to get very cold after a strenuous effort)
shorts/tights or **half tights**	Please see the section on clothing to determine which is right for you.
warm-up suit or **tights**	Unless it is summer, you will need to cover up after your race.
8 safety pins	• 4 to pin your number on your jersey • 4 for an absent-minded runner, or friend who will have forgotten theirs
toilet paper	Nerves tend to speed up the intestinal tract, so be prepared!
old newspaper	This gives you something to stand on when you are changing shoes, so you don't get dirty. Also good for wrapping up dirty shoes after the race on a wet day.
blister kit Vaseline, 'second skin' or other protective dressing, needle and matches, sterile gauze pads, disinfectant of choice	Please see the section 'blisters' to see how to attend to any blisters you may acquire through running a long distance event.
plastic rubbish bag	• may be used as a disposable wind-jacket if you should need to stand around on the starting line • comes in handy for transporting wet clothing and shoes

Figure 20: Race day check list

Object	Comments
toilet articles towel, soap, shampoo, brush, fresh bra/panties	You don't know if a warm shower will be available, but if it is, you will feel much better for having taken one before heading home again. Be prepared, just in case!
snack food dry fruit, biscuits or crackers, 'power bars' or similar, energy drink	The sooner you tank up after the end of your race, the sooner you will replace your glycogen stores. (see chapter six)
racing shoes	After you start racing seriously, you may choose to race in lighter-weight racing shoes.

Figure 20: Race day check list (cont)

completely to drink without losing much time out of the race, or you can try to drink on the run without getting water up your nose. The more humid the weather, the more important it is for you to drink. You may also pour extra water over your head, and down your back to help cool your body. In longer races, such as the half marathon or anything longer, you must drink, regardless of the weather. If you wait until you are thirsty, you have already waited too long. Thirst is not a good indicator. You must drink before you get to that point. Eat if you are hungry, or feeling weak, as these may be signs of hypoglycaemia.

After the race

Unless it is very hot, change clothes quickly after the finish line. Change your bra if you can, put on a dry t-shirt, and a warm-up jacket. Walk around a bit, rehydrate and nourish yourself. You will need lots of fluids during the day following the race, and you can eat whatever suits you, although you may tolerate only easy-to-digest foods. Take a warm shower as soon as you can, and finally, put your feet up. You deserve it!

BRANCHING OUT
Cross-training, triathlons, diversifying and more!

I remember my first duathlon. It consisted of running 3 kms, biking 16 and then running 3 more kms. I had a great time for the first 3 kms. The biking was a totally new experience. I was not very efficient to start with, but then I got into a groove (even though I had to fight against putting on the brakes every time I went downhill!). I had a different kind of interaction with the other competitors. The last 3 km run was yet another awakening! I had rubbery 'bike legs' and had to adjust and find strength and balance I didn't know I had. A lovely woman, fifteen years my senior, who finished right on my heels, gently prompted me. 'You'll be surprised how much good this does your running. You should do duathlons more often!'

Jeni D. (30, psychologist)

Running makes me feel strong. My muscles are well defined and I feel powerful. When running, I feel like I know my body, and I can use it. Your body starts working for you and you develop a bond with it.

Running can introduce you to a new world of fitness that contains much, much more than just stride after stride. Your legs are stronger, your cardio-vascular system more efficient, and other sports may naturally seem more attractive than they did before you started running. Cross-training (or training by the use of complementary sports) has definite advantages that are worth thinking about.

You can introduce almost any other kind of sport training into your running programme, and gain benefit. It can keep you from going 'stale', or losing interest, on those days when you might not be motivated to run, but could envisage going for a ride or a swim, with less aversion. You may gain a psychological boost from changing environments. On a hot day on holiday a swim in the lake may be more appealing than another road run. You can also develop skills and conditioning which will help your running. Many multi-sporters will tell you how their 10 km times improved when they started training for the triathlon, even though they reduced the amount of running they were doing. Finally, and perhaps, most importantly, you can use complementary activities as a way of preventing overuse injuries. If pounding the pavement is taking its toll, you might try replacing two of your runs during the week with a pool or a bike session. You will get off your feet, and use different muscle groups. Biking and swimming are excellent alternative activities while recovering from injury as well.

Training on the bike

Biking is an attractive alternative to running. When it is cold and windy outside, you can bike on a wind-trainer, or a stationary bike. When it is hot and humid, biking provides you with a much better breeze than when running. If you are going to bike, make sure that your bike is properly adjusted, that the saddle is at the right height, and that your handlebars are correctly positioned. The local bike shop should be able to help you with this. If you are planning on cycling regularly, and if your budget allows, outfit your bike with a cycle computer, so that you can monitor your pedal cadence, and toe-clips.

Choose a route which is safe, meaning not too many huge trucks barrelling through with no regard to slower vehicles, but also one where wind exposure is not too severe. As a less-than-expert cyclist, I know that it is already hard enough to stick to the road, let alone with a 40 knot wind to challenge you! Protected routes are desirable.

When you are cycling, concentrate not only on pushing down the pedals, but also on pulling them back up again, on the upstroke. You will thus use your calves and hamstrings, as opposed to just your quads. Your pedal cadence should be much faster than you might expect. You should pedal at 80–90 revolutions per minute. You may slow down slightly on the hills, but if you drop below 75, you should change gears to allow you to keep up the faster rhythm. You may find that your heart rate does not climb as high when you are biking, as when you are running. Try to maintain a steady level of exertion, and make sure you bike for at least 45 minutes each session.

Swimming

Swimming won't necessarily make you run faster, but it will certainly improve your upper body conditioning, and it will provide you with a lovely horizontal exercise position, with all the gravity-countering advantages that entails.

The best way to succeed with a swimming programme is to get a coach or instructor for your first sessions, to make sure that you are using proper form and obtaining the most from your sessions. You can do laps, intervals, or kick drills. As with running, you can do repetitions while swimming. For example, you might swim 10 x 100 metres, with a 2 minute rest between each repetition. Or, you might try a kind of fartlek; swimming laps, with a harder surge every second or third lap.

Depending on where you live you can also vary the type of swimming you do. You can swim in a lake, in the sea or in an outdoor pool. Make sure that you have learned water safety skills, and that you

> Theresa H. (38, registered nurse, 4 children)
>
> I have been running for about ten years. Everyone in the family is involved in running. I always go first thing in the morning. If I don't go at 6am, I won't find the time. It's not that I am fanatically disciplined, or anything. I used to be a swimmer, and that got me used to training early in the morning.

are buddied for non-pool swimming. Safety first!

Weight training

I enjoy going to the gym. It is one of the only places where I can watch people exercising, and feel a sense of belonging to a larger set of fitness buffs. The clinking sound of weights jangling, the smell of liniment and, yes, hot bodies, really gets me pumping! The first time in a new gym is always the worst. I walk in, and see people lifting twice my body weight, as if there were nothing to it, and I put two 10 kg disks on the bar for my own work. Confidence does come rapidly, and it becomes a great place to train. Weight training is excellent exercise for general fitness, and especially for bone fitness. Studies, including post-menopausal women, have shown the advantages that weight training can offer for creating strong, hard bones.

If you are a bit intimidated about going to the gym for the first time, you might try to find a friend to go along with you. There has recently been more awareness about women's need to have a place of their own to train, and a number of gyms are 'women only' or have 'women only' hours. Enquire in your area.

If you do not have experience in weight training, make an appointment for your first session with someone who will show you the equipment, and, if you wish, work out a personal programme for you. This should be a one-off expense, and is often included in a membership fee. You may wish to go one step further and hire a personal trainer to follow you for the first few weeks and advise you on ways to make your gym sessions more successful. This is not usually essential, but can be helpful if you wish further guidance.

It is good to pair up with someone for your weight sessions, because some exercises require a spotter (someone to help guide the weights as a safety procedure). If you go to train with a friend, you will be well set-up, but most weight trainers are more than happy to spot for each other.

I think that only limited lower body work is necessary for a recreational runner. Your leg strength is probably adequately developed through running alone. You may find that some complementary exercises are helpful (i.e.: calf raises are wonderful, if you tend to get achilles tendonitis). On the other hand, you can get in a lot of beneficial upper body work in the weight room. Your trainer will be able to help you define which exercises will be best for you. Do keep in mind the fact that as an endurance athlete, you will probably want to do a relatively high number of lifts, with relatively low weight.

It is hard to run after a good weight

session. I prefer to have a light run beforehand.

Fitting it all in

If you run, swim, bike and lift every week, how in the world can you fit it all in? Well, you probably want to alternate. You can run every other day, and fit in complementary exercise on the off days. You can also pair up a run and a swim once or twice a week (e.g.: park at the pool, run for 30 minutes, then swim for 30 minutes), or do the same with a weights or aerobic session (go for a light 30 minute run, weight room or aerobics for 30 minutes). If you wish to pair up the run and the bike, try the run first. Jumping off a bike to go for a run gives you a 'rubbery leg' sensation which is hard to overcome.

CHAPTER FOUR

The Running Woman and the Outside World

SOME HISTORICAL BACKGROUND[6]

When I started running, in 1973, running itself was an oddity, much less women's running. At that time, there was only one running magazine available in Charlottesville, Virginia, and only three copies were sent to the *Dixie News*, the only news-stand that received it. In order to make sure I got my copy, I had to dash down at the first of the month, and hope no one had arrived before me.

I had become involved in running almost by accident. A lanky, 5′ 7″ ninth grader, I had tried out for the school basketball team, and failed to be selected. It was a blow, for although I knew I was more awkward than many of my peers, I had thought that my

height would have been adequate to gain me a spot on the squad. Being successful in athletics was important to me, given the emphasis on sport in my school. Not discouraged, I thought about what else I might be able to do. 'Well, I could always run...'

When try-outs for the track team were announced over the school's public announcement system later that month, I made my decision. I would run track. Of course, I knew well that the team for which try-outs were being held was the *boys'* track team, but it was the decade of statements. I intended to make my own statement, and with six or seven other girls, I appeared on the first day of track practice. Firmly, we were told that this was the *boys'* team, and that girls couldn't practise. Obediently, most of the girls went home. The two of us who remained managed to change the coaches' minds, and ran our first successful track season. We would go on to win the mixed 440

---

6 There are some lovely books on the history of sport, and of women's sport. Check the 'Recommended Reading' section.

yard relay at the state invitational meet. I continued running in cross-country, on another 'all-boys' team.

My ability to work my way into a boys' (men's) sport had not been easy. Other real pioneers had earlier set the example of what women were capable of doing. Going back to mythical times, Atlanta, a Greek maiden, agreed to marry the man who could outrun her. Unfortunately for her suitors, she raced too quickly, and killed her suitors with bow and arrow. She finally was overtaken by Hippomenes, who dropped golden apples in her pathway, which she paused to gather.

The original Olympic Games were reserved for men. In fact, women were not even allowed to watch the activities under threat of death. On the other hand, a similar festival of sport is thought to have taken place in the ancient Greek city of Elis and attracted women from all over Greece. The running event was open to young women who ran in their age-groups. They wore short tunics which revealed their right breast. These girls ran $5/6$ of the distance covered by the men. Some scholars have suggested these races may have been part of pre-nuptial rites.

In eighteenth century Great Britain, scantily-clad country girls would participate in 'Smock Races'. These events took place for the entertainment of rowdy townspeople, and the winner of the event – wearing little more than a pair of drawers – would win a smock, and possibly even a spouse, for her efforts. In the nineteenth, and more moralistic, century, women were discouraged from running and leaping, due to the 'excessive shocks'. There was a Victorian fear that athletics would damage the female reproductive organs, and that women runners would be unable to fulfill their womanly duty of conception and motherhood. In 1859, in South Australia, a ladies' race was announced, but the outcry was such that it was cancelled. By 1903 however, 2500 Paris shop girls took part in a 12 km run from the Place de la Concorde to Nanterre, and Jeanne Cheminel finished first in 1 hour and 10 minutes. The next year, in Germany, 70 women competed in the Damensportfest in Berlin. They participated in 400 metre heats, and a 500 metre final.

Francoise L. *(71. Started running at age 55. Won the world age group record for the 6 day run – 403 miles for ages 60–64, and tenth best performance of all time, all ages, for the 48-hour run, at age 62!)*

When I married at 23 years of age, my mother made sure that sport did not interfere with my motherhood. I was to avoid all jolts which might be incompatible with pregnancy. The noble role of motherhood left no room for sport. My job was to re-populate the nation! Of course, in those days, I agreed.

Progressively, the twentieth century saw an acceptance, and then a true belief, in the advantage of running for women.

In 1928, women's track and field was introduced at the Olympics in Amsterdam, despite fears that 'feminine muscular development would interfere with motherhood'. Such athletes as Babe Didrickson, Fanny Blankers-Koen, Wilma Rudolph and Betty Cuthbert would grace the world scene and call attention to the athletic ability of women in running.

In more recent times, Roberta Gibb, in 1966, completed the Boston Marathon. Although she was not officially entered in the event, she covered the distance, in a respectable time of 3 hours 20 minutes. Even as recently as that, observers were surprised to think that a woman could actually run so far. The following year, Kathrine Switzer entered the running scene with a loud bang. A young university student in the late 1960s, Switzer was a runner. She ran in the days prior to the running fad. She had competed, albeit slowly, on the men's university team, and most of all, she thrived on running long distances. She had noticed that even though her speed was well under that of the men she ran with, she could outlast many of them. She trained in Syracuse, New York. One of her training partners was a 50-year-old postman named Arnie Briggs. Arnie had run many marathons, and liked to talk about them. He had run the Boston Marathon fifteen times. On their long winter runs, Arnie would go on and on about this marathon and that marathon. Kathrine listened to his stories, and one day proclaimed that she too wanted to run a marathon. Even though they had covered many miles together (more than many men who trained for marathons), Arnie was dubious, if not downright sceptical. Kathrine was convinced she was capable, and Arnie said, 'If you can cover the distance in practice, I'll take you to Boston!' So in the cold Syracuse winter of 1966, Kathrine Switzer made one small decision which would later be of enormous consequence: she started training for her first marathon. There were four months to go before the famed marathon. Every weekend, the duo would go for longer and longer outings, and finally, three weeks prior to the big event, they ran the magical distance. They had a series of loop circuits of varying lengths. At the end of the 26-mile run, Kathrine, in order to convince herself for once and for all that she was not only capable, but more than capable, of running a full marathon, decided to tack on an extra 5-mile loop. Arnie followed. A mile from the end, Arnie started hallucinating. His legs were getting rubbery. When they finally finished together, Kathrine, in her elation, started squealing, 'We did it! We did it!' Her running partner had fainted dead away. When he came to, he was convinced. Kathrine was indeed more than capable of covering the distance. Arnie procured entry forms, and both runners had the then-required medical examinations performed, and they entered the race: A. Briggs and K.V. Switzer.

When Kathrine told her boyfriend that she was going to run the Boston Marathon, he guffawed. 'Women can't run marathons!' he laughed. She explained that he might not think women could run marathons, but that she, Kathrine Switzer, could and would run a marathon in Boston the following month. A second little event took place, that would also be of great retrospective importance: her boyfriend, Tom Miller, national calibre hammer thrower, put in his entry. 'If you're going to Boston, so am I!' he proclaimed.

The rest is history. Kathrine, Tom and Arnie went to Boston as members of the Syracuse Harriers. Kathrine couldn't wait to run. The elation of having completed a 31 mile training run had her on a cloud. She wanted to get to Boston to 'strut her stuff'. Race day dawned cold and drizzly. Kathrine was wearing a hooded warm-up jacket, and grotty old training pants. It was cold. The men around her could see that she

was a woman, but deep in the masses, no one really cared. The race organiser, Jock Semple, actually put his hand on her shoulder and shoved her towards the starting pen. He didn't notice that she was not a man. The thought probably never crossed his mind that a woman might try to run the race.

As it was her first marathon, she started cautiously, with her two running partners. The press truck started in the very back, and as it worked its way forward, the journalists noticed that the slight figure in the grey warm-up suit was a woman. Not only was she a woman, she was wearing an official number. The press started goading Jock Semple about having a 'broad' in his race.

It is hard work to organise a marathon, and Semple was probably under more pressure than he would like to admit. The needling got to him, his temper was hot, and he committed the act which would go down in history as the affront to women runners that catalysed their integration into world running, and eventually into the Olympic marathon. Semple jumped off the press truck and ran after Switzer in order to stop her. And then all of a sudden, a streak of Syracuse orange (team colours) came full tilt at him. It was Tom! He took out Jock with a shoulder block, and swept him right off his feet! Fortunately for women's running, this event took place in full view of the photographers and journalists. The photos would grace the front pages of all the national papers the next morning: *Chivalry is not Dead!, Woman Runs Boston Marathon!* These photos would immortalise the event, driving home the blatantly chauvinistic attitude of the race organiser, and highlighting Switzer's ability to run with the men. It tuned the public in to the situation that existed in women's sports in general, and running in particular.

The media impact of this incident was great. Switzer used what she had learned and experienced to campaign for inclusion of women in long distance events. By 1972, women were allowed, for the first time, to run the Boston Marathon officially. At the 1972 New York Marathon, the following autumn, they were allowed to run, but only if they started separately from the men. A sit-in occurred, where the women protested the separate starts, and finally, the Amateur Athletic Union authorised women to run the same races, at the same time, as men. Only the results would be separated. In 1972, only two women were able to run faster than three hours for the marathon. In 1994, 30 women ran 2h 30 or better! The advances have been monumental. From 1500 metres in 1980, to 42.195 kilometres in 1984, the longest distance that women could run was finally increased to reflect the ability of women

to run the same races as men. Joan Benoit would ultimately show the way to women of the world in the first women's Olympic marathon.

By 1994, three women had broken 2:22 for the marathon distance. Media attention, and prize money for women is starting to match that given to men. There is a financial incentive for top women track runners to transfer their skills to the long distance road running events, which leads to great hope for future performance levels.

WHY DO MEN RUN FASTER THAN WOMEN?

Why do men run faster than women? I have run for more than two thirds of my life. When I started, at age 13, I was the only girl on the team. I was surprised that I was able to train with them without looking silly, and even beat many of them when I ran the high school cross-country races. I had reached my adult height and weight, and could run circles around some of the males of my age, who were still little boys. I was, by far, the most dedicated runner on the team. They all teased me about how serious I was. As I grew older, I trained more and more, and the same young boys had their growth spurts, looked more like men, and started to outrun me. Of course, I still run much faster than most men, even experienced

runners, but there remains a barrier that separates the men from the women that I can't erase. Men are, simply put, better equipped than women for running. The world athletic records are the proof. Florence Griffith-Joyner's barely believable 10.49 seconds for 100m (world record in 1993) is more than 7% inferior to the male record, and this difference is even greater in most events: usually almost 10%. There are hundreds of men in the world who can run faster than Tegla Loroupe, who holds the women's world record for the marathon.

What do they have that we don't? Let's look at some of the factors which make men better runners on race day. We can start by looking at the issue from a sociological standpoint. In studies which observe pre-pubescent boys and girls, it was shown that the boys were barely stronger than the girls in tests of speed, endurance, or agility.[7] On the other hand, in tests of comparative skill in areas which have been considered 'boy' sports (in this case, the baseball throw), girls were significantly less adept. After the girls were coached in baseball throwing, the difference in ability vanished. The male advantage, in this case, came from the emphasis placed on throwing sports for boys and not on any real difference in ability. After adolescence, however, boys

7 Wilmore 1981.

> 'Psychologically, men are more often explosive, inconstant, not enduring and in pain and exertion – especially among high performance athletes – somewhat snivelling. Woman is the opposite: tough, constant, enduring, level and calm under endurance exertion and the pain to which her biology exposes her (childbearing) …Armed with these advantages, women are in a position to do endurance feats previously considered impossible.'
>
> Ernst van Aaken (1976) as quoted in *The Lore of Running* by Tim Noakes.

performed better than girls in all areas, confirming what I had noticed on the training fields as a teenage participant. It is, of course, during adolescence that 'play' is exchanged for 'sport'. Sport is an important part of male development, but is played down for females.

This neglect has been reinforced for years by the international governing bodies of track and field. Women have only been allowed to run middle and long distance events for a short time. We remember the first Olympic marathon, won brilliantly by the determined, and yes, feminine, Joan Benoit in 1984. It was at those same games that the 3000 metres was introduced. Until then, the longest distance women were allowed to run was only 1500m (less than a mile)! Women were excluded from longer races because of a decision dating back to the Amsterdam Olympics in 1928.

Women were allowed to run the 800 metres at those games, but an unreasonable schedule of heats and finals on the same day left many of the women exhausted. Instead of rescheduling the events for future Olympics, the International Olympic Committee (all male) decided simply to eliminate that event from the games. It was not to be run again until the Rome games in 1960. The 400 metres reappeared in Tokyo, four years later.

Education and international recognition are not the only factors which keep women behind men at all levels of competition. Men are taller and heavier than women. The wider pelvis of women rotates more, reducing stride efficiency. Women have, on average, twice as much body fat as men, and subsequently they have less muscle mass. Even a very well-trained woman will have 15% less muscle fibres than in a similarly trained man. The VO_2 Max, or the body's ability to transport and use oxygen, is influenced by these differences, because fatty tissues are not as highly vascularised as muscle tissue, and hence, cannot use oxygen as well. Oxygen is the fuel for athletic activity. With higher muscle mass, men also have more ATP, the enzyme required for muscle contraction to take place.

Men's cardio-vascular systems are also better suited to performance. The blood volume is greater in men than in women.

The heart chambers are larger, as is the amount of blood ejected with each beat. Men have higher haemoglobin levels. Haemoglobin is the iron containing pigment of the red blood cells whose function it is to transport oxygen. The loss of menstrual blood in women further reduces their haemoglobin level, and thus, their ability to oxygenate their muscles in running events.

Testosterone, a male hormone, increases the metabolic rate, and enables recovery after intense exercise to take place more quickly. Testosterone also contributes to compact, powerful muscles, and other secondary male characteristics, such as the deepening of the voice, and body hair. Although all women have a measurable amount of testosterone in their blood, it is minimal compared with that of men. Many of the known illegal performance enhancing substances are derived from these hormones. The effects of artificially absorbed male hormones can be particularly obvious (though not always). In a woman, this may be seen by a masculinisation reflected by highly defined and compact muscles, male body hair, acne, psychological (going as far as full psychosis) and sexual problems, including loss of libido.

So it might appear that women should just throw in the towel. They have the cards stacked against them from the start! Well, let's start by pointing out that we needn't compare. Let's also point out the incomparable life styles of men and women, especially if the women are both bread-earners and mothers. Sports journalists who give female athletes as much attention as males will help contribute to the breaking down of social prejudices. Race organisers who focus on providing the same support and incentives to women runners as they do to men also do much for the cause of women's running.

And the issue is not as simple as the best women versus the best men. There is intense competition within the women's running world, and good women can compete favourably against many men. Ann Trason, famed American ultra-distance runner, races and beats international-calibre male runners over distances such as 50 miles, 100km and longer. She is also a tremendous off-road runner. Off-road running requires the use not only of physiological abilities, but of perseverance and other psychological skills. Women have often been thought to have more stamina than men, or a better ability to run longer races due to a wider pelvis and greater fat reserves. Fat is a rich source of energy for events of long duration. These assumptions have yet to be scientifically proven, but are worthy of research.

Women, even those less talented than Ann Trason, are still competitive. The leading women runners in international road races are always surrounded by male competitors, drafting off the often more experienced female runner. The same thing happens at all levels of competition. Whether you run 5km in 15 minutes, or in 25, or in more, you'll never be running alone!

So, while we can't necessarily run as fast as the best men, we can continue to optimise our ability. It is great to be a woman, and women *can* run!

THE DEFENSIVE ART OF RUNNING ALONE

Running alone can be a great pleasure: away from the frivolous (though sometimes enjoyable) chitchat of group runs, alone with the freedom to run at any pace, to crawl, if need be, or to fly over the hills, without being chided about 'racing' away from the party, or holding it up. Alone to savour the silence. No phones ringing, no questions to answer, no children to take care of. Running on your own offers an opportunity to get in touch with your self, and your body. I love to run with my friends, club mates, and training partners. But I truly savour a few runs a week on my own. That is when I do much of the psychological preparation for upcoming races. It is easy to visualise racing outcomes while running, or to focus my attention on whatever my current goal is, with the rhythmic turnover of my stride methodically hammering it into place: 2:45, 2:45, 2:45, 2:45 . . . It is also when I think out my articles, and work out complicated work issues.

Running safely when alone

Many women feel exceedingly vulnerable when they go for a run on their own. Others feel perfectly safe. Actually, both positions are mistaken. As females, it would be wrong to think that the world is a perfectly safe place. It isn't. Some men choose to attack women, and few of us are properly prepared physically or psychologically to defend ourselves.

Even though I can run a half marathon, my legs are no match over a short sprint for many men, especially if I am taken by surprise! By training at all hours of the day or night, I might seem to be tempting fate. Does that mean that

I am destined to be a victim? No way! That is where defensive running has its place.

You may not live in a troubled area, or in a big city, but female runners are harassed and both physically and verbally assaulted in all parts of the world – rural, as well as urban – and no place is exempt. Female runners are exposed to a greater risk than one might imagine. They may exercise in isolated areas, and they have

predictable patterns of behaviour: finish work at five-thirty, change clothes at the gym, on the tracks by six o'clock, every day except for weekends.

To make running alone safe, it is important to follow a few rules, and to keep the idea of safety paramount. Not only is assault, be it verbal or physical, of concern. It is important to realise than any hitch along the way becomes more serious when you are alone, be it a turned ankle, a vicious dog, a change in the weather, or simply a wrong turn far from home. The 'rules' listed here address these issues as well:

1. Let your partner, room-mate, mum or next door neighbour know where you are going and for how long, before you take off for your run. If you live on your own, jot down your planned course, and leave the note on your kitchen table.

2. Choose your running course carefully. It is a good idea to vary the route, and the time of your run, so that no one can anticipate your moves. If you must run in the dark, choose well-lit, well-populated areas. Be cautious about isolated tracks at all times. Even simple things like turning an ankle become more complicated when you are on your own, so save your mountain track runs to do with company.

3. Take some small change and a phone card with you. If you are alone, and run into trouble, like an ankle sprain, or hypoglycaemia, you could use a pay phone, buy a chocolate bar, solve some of the easier problems.

4. Carry some identification when you run alone in isolated areas. In case you do run into trouble, and are unable to identify yourself, you'll be taken care of. If you have any medical problems, medication allergies, diabetes, make sure that you wear either a medic alert bracelet, or carry some form of written information to be used in case of accident. One of my running partners has a resting heart rate of 38. It has been explored, and is normal for him. It would be a shame for him to be given intensive cardiac inotropic drugs when not needed. I hope he carries that information on him when he runs.

5. Be alert when you run. Do not wear a Walkman (and I mean *never*!). Protect your side flanks by running close to a wall, or shop fronts. Keep your identification or valuables to the protected side. Should you be running in a forest, keep close to the side of the track which would provide the most difficult access for a potential attacker. Stay away from large bushes and concealed areas, parked vans and the like.

6. Look tough. Run like you mean it. Avoid making eye contact, which may be misinterpreted. On the other hand, should there be a confrontation, do not take your eyes off your attacker for a second. His head will always move before his feet, and this will help you to anticipate his movement.

7. Carry a screech alarm, if you wish. It may serve to raise the alarm to nearby houses or passersby. But think of the screech alarm as part of your self-defence armoury, not as a protection in itself.

8. If you are attacked, remember where your strength lies: in your legs and in your brain. Get angry. Attackers expect you to scream and panic. Fighting back and yelling angrily gives you the immediate advantage of surprise, and can be enough to ward off many attackers. Kick his testicles as hard as you can, whenever possible. There is no pain as immediately debilitating as this for a man. Aim also for the front of his legs and knees. If your arms are free go for his eyes and throat. Don't scream – turn it into a deep angry yell from your stomach and let fly! Do anything you can to avoid getting into a car, and never give up.

9. Consider taking a self-defence course. Make sure you check the course out thoroughly. Do you feel comfortable with the instructor? Do you know anyone who has taken the course and are they satisfied with their instruction? One agency I called has a flat fee for the course, and the lessons are conducted until the client feels she has mastered the skill of self-defence completely. Others run women-only classes with female instructors. Do the techniques seem to match your need? Some of the eastern methods are not necessarily adapted to western violence.

10. Run with a dog (a big one!). People will think twice before bothering you then!

Far from wanting to dissuade any woman from running, or from running on her own, I hope that these recommendations may help to prevent active athletic women from being seen as suitable targets for criminal attacks. Safety first!

RUNNING WITH MEN

'What me? Go running with men? Never! I would prefer to go training at midnight, so no one can see me! I couldn't run with a man! What's more, what man would run as slowly as I do?!'

This may be the way you are feeling right now. If you have been running on your own, or in the company of other beginning women runners, the idea of running with men might be amongst the scariest of ideas I have put forth yet. I really wanted to introduce this thought, because there are such plentiful running partners amongst the male population that it is worthy of discussion. Perhaps I should start by pointing out that I have almost never seen a woman be the last runner to cross the finish line in a race. Men do run slowly too. Furthermore, those who are running slowly are far more concerned with their own desire to run, get fit, commune with nature, etc., than they are with what you look like and how fast you run. You will always be more judgmental with regards to yourself than the people who run with you will be.

Men are great training partners, no matter what your training speed is. If you feel pretty confident about your running ability and pace, you will find that male training partners may help you to attain a higher level of exertion. If you are a slower, put-in-the-miles-but-do-it-gently kind of person, having some company will make the time fly, and there are more men out there running than there are women! Furthermore, if you must run before sunrise, or after dark, running with a man can make you feel more secure. But, when all this is said and done, there are some things to keep in mind.

Be confident of your ability to judge your pace. If it feels too fast, don't do it! One of the most common things about taking a run with someone you've never run with before (male or female), is that you both come away from that first run exhausted. Why? Well, you said to yourself, 'Gee, he looks relaxed. This must be his training pace (puff). I don't want to hold him back!' He on the other hand, was in all likelihood saying to himself 'Wow! She runs fast! She looks relaxed. This must be her training pace! (puff, puff).' It always happens! We are constantly judging people's outsides by our insides ('he *looks* good'; 'I *feel* bad'). If we knew how they *felt*, we would probably not be so likely to follow their external cues. So, on a first run with someone new, try saying, 'Is this your usual training pace? Do you mind if we slow it down a bit?'

Most men *do* have more experience exercising than women. That is how society has guided us all these years. That doesn't mean, necessarily, that they know more about you, or about what you should be doing, than you do. I have found that I must occasionally defend myself from an insecure male ego, who in an attempt to feel more confident about his own ability, showers me with advice that is relatively useless. I smile and keep going. I know where I am going, and so do you. That doesn't mean that the advice from an experienced runner who has much to offer should be disregarded. It just means that you should make sure you have the right messenger before you heed the message.

Should men train more rapidly than women? Not necessarily. When I was the female provincial champion in road running, my times were about 12% slower than the male champion and this remains the rule generally. That doesn't keep us from training together, and quite easily. I wouldn't do a speed session on the track, or even a sustained run, with him, and hope to keep him in sight. On the other hand, our easy runs are generally quite close in pace. Racing pace and ability do not necessarily dictate training run pace. So, I (and you too) can train, even with men who are much faster than you when they race.

The discrepancy in ability levels is sometimes very frustrating. Time after time, I find a good male training partner, who, after following the same focused training, will achieve much better performances than I. We may have started running together at a similar pace, even for the fast work, but as the months go by, that male runner makes much more improvement than I, and leaves me behind. Sigh. We have to work with what we have, and the gender related performance differences cannot be erased, even by hard work. On the other hand, having a faster male training partner can be very convenient. As I write these words, I am thinking about the work-out I have planned for later this week. It is one of my 'dreaded' work-outs, as it is not my forté at all. I have planned to run a 5km 'strong run'. That means I will run much harder than regular training pace, for a long time. I have trouble focusing on such work-outs, and I don't always do as well as I would like to. But I have asked one of the better local male runners if he wouldn't mind setting the pace for me for the first half of the strong run. For him it is easy to run a 5km in 17 minutes, whereas I have to psych myself up and really push hard. This work-out is going to be a lot easier, because all I will have to do is settle in behind him, and let him take the wind and pull me along.

Of course, I should also mention how women can help men. Many a man has been eager to run a work-out with me, or with other women, because experience has nothing to do with gender. I have plenty of experience with running, and that can help my training partners, men and women alike. So do you! You may know a course that your running partners have never been on, you may have already run your first race, whereas a beginning male runner has

not. Sometimes there are less pressures on a woman to 'perform' when they undertake their first race. There is perhaps a greater perceived risk of failure for men, and the different approach of some women can be helpful.

Although many men have been ungracious about being beaten by me in competition, many too have been gallant and respectful. One memory I have cherished of men and women helping each other to run is pertinent here. In my first year of harrier running at my high school, as the only girl on the team, I prepared for the first home meet. John Connelly was a big seventeen-year-old boy, who was running cross-country to stay in shape for some high profile sport (I don't remember which). He suspected that I was probably capable of running faster than he, even though I was a girl, and only fourteen. As I was warming up, I jogged over to talk to him, as we usually enjoyed training together. Rather surprisingly, John said, 'I need to be on my own. I am afraid you are going to beat me, and I have to stay away from you right now.' I respectfully gave him space. Indeed, I went out faster than he did, and appeared to be the stronger runner. Coming down a little dip, however, I tripped and fell. In frustration, I started to walk, and meant to drop out of the race. John came up from behind. Although his greatest fear was to be beaten by a girl, he gave me a push. 'Don't quit!' he admonished, and he got me back on track...So that I could beat him! I have not forgotten how he helped me.

To summarise, it is great to be able to run, and to have company while exercising. Men make wonderful partners for a jog, a run, a speed session, or a race – and they will be thankful for your company too.

DOGS

A dog can be your best friend, but a stranger's dog can be an unwelcome foe, as you go out for your regular runs. Yours can help you out by keeping those with bad intentions out of your path. But, an unknown dog can come snarling up at your ankles when you run by their territory.

The aggressive dog and the runner

Some delightfully friendly dogs can turn into snarling monsters when they think you are threatening their property, or their owners. For some reason, gentle runners look like wicked villains to many dogs, and the sound of your pitter-pattering feet will drive them insane! Many runners have scars from dog bites to show for their isolated country runs. If you meet a dog that you don't know while out on a run:

– Look for its owner, and make sure that they notice your arrival. That will give them time to call the dog before you run by.
– If the owner is not in sight, slow down to a walk and try to assess the animal. If it seems friendly, speak to it kindly. Reassure it that you mean no harm, and walk by the property. If, on the other hand, the dog growls or appears hostile, you have a few options.

1) Take a detour, or turn back, if that is possible, and the dog is not yet on your heels.
2) Be assertive, shouting at the animal, 'Go away!' as loudly as you can, and pretending to throw something at it. A veterinarian/triathlete friend of mine swears that will work. I haven't tried this tactic, which is nonetheless based on an excellent understanding of animal behaviour. Do not stare at the animal, as this can be seen as a challenge to the dog, but keep it in sight, so that you can try to anticipate its moves. Above all, try to control your own fear.
3) Don't turn your back on the dog. Walk, or run backwards, again, keeping the animal in sight.
4) If you are bitten, or attacked, seek medical attention immediately. If there are any witnesses, or neighbours, speak to them, and see if they know who owns the dog. You will

need to be in touch with the owners to obtain vaccination information about their dog. They also must be counselled to keep closer control of their pet.

Running with your dog

A dog can make a wonderful running partner. Not all dogs are made to run long distances however. Dogs with heavy bone structure may have joint problems if you try to turn them into long distance runners. Dobermans, poodles, setters, and Dalmatians are all good running dogs. Many mutts are not. Check with your veterinarian before you take your dog out running with you. Your dog will need to work into running, if it has not been exercising beyond the standard walk-around-the-block until now. Start your dog running with short runs, like you did when you first started. It will probably take less time for the dog to get fit, because it may not have indulged in the same kinds of excesses as people can (cigarettes, alcohol, sedentary life-style...). The problem is that the dog cannot give you feedback as to how it is feeling. Dogs are so loyal, that they will just keep running until they drop. With that thought in mind, it is good to be prudent. If your animal seems lazy, or hard to rouse for your daily run, it may be saying 'This is too much for me right now!' so go off on your own instead.

Keep an eye on the dog's paws. Avoid running on rocky surfaces which may hurt its feet. You can buy products to help toughen the pads. Check with the vet on this. When it is hot out, be doubly careful with your dog. Dogs do not have as many means to regulate their inside temperature as humans do. Their resting temperature is already higher than that of humans. Make sure there is plenty of cool water available on your running course, and take special care to observe your dog, and keep it cool. An overheated dog will show the same symptoms as an overheated person (see 'Overheating' later in this chapter), and will need to be cooled down rapidly, with water. Drenching the dog with water will assist in this, but never *sponge* a long-haired dog – the damp surface will trap the heat under the coat. Seek veterinary assistance immediately if your dog overheats.

Make sure your dog is obedient, and will stay with you while you are running. It is in the interest of its own safety, and of that of other runners. A big (friendly) dog can give another runner a fright. I have run with friends whose dogs have almost caused me harm in their enthusiasm to get up to their owner, nearly toppling me in their path. So, make sure your dog either knows the rules of the road (unlikely), or is on a lead.

RUNNING FOR ALL SEASONS
Winter running

In most cases, you don't have to stop running just because it is cold outside. It would be a shame to have to give up running because of a cold snap. You can prepare yourself for winter in such a way that running is possible, but very carefully. Mistakes can be fatal!

The human body is not well-designed to adapt to the cold. Although we can sweat to cool off when the outside temperature is high, we have no similar cold weather protection. Of course, we get goose-bumps, we shiver, and our peripheral circulation tightens up in order to keep good blood flow and warmth to our important central organs, but that doesn't do much good for protection against the cold while running. It is up to us, then, to plan a strategy of cold protection in order to make winter running possible. Let's look at the principal areas of heat loss while running, in order to see what measures are most important to keep it to a minimum.

Internal energy production continues to take place, regardless of the outside temperature. This means that you will perspire, despite the fact that it is cold outside. Having moist skin or clothing can accelerate heat loss by **evaporation**. As you run, you create air movement which enhances heat loss by **convection**. This is particularly true in the presence of wind, but remains a factor even without windy conditions. And finally, well-vascularised but poorly covered parts of the body, such as the head and face, allow the **radiation** of heat, and further chilling of the runner. In order to run in the winter, the effects of evaporation, convection and radiation must be countered.

Before you go for a run in the winter, make sure you know what the weather is like. Many cases of extreme hypothermia are due simply to ill-preparation. If you get caught in a downpour without proper rain gear, a 7°C day can become potentially dangerously cold. Don't just look at the thermometer to decide what to wear. Consider as well, the amount of wind, how strong it is, and the risk of rain. Dress accordingly. You will need clothing that will keep you dry, and that will

Wind (mph)	30	20	10	0	–01	–20
0	30	20	10	0	–10	–20
10	16	4	–9	–24	–33	–46
20	4	–10	–25	–39	–53	–67
30	–2	–18	–33	–48	–63	–78
40	–6	–21	–37	–53	–69	–86

The non-shaded zones show how much the wind contributes to cooling. It is important to note that, even though the chart deals primarily with freezing temperatures, wind can be dangerous in much milder weather. A 10 or 15 degree day can become perilous rapidly if the wind or rain enter into play.

Figure 21: Outside temperature °C

prevent heat loss by convection or radiation. There are many new textiles available on the market for runners who need protection from the winter weather. Unfortunately, they are all fairly expensive, but I'd say that most of them are worth the investment. One set of **polypropylene** undergear is the best investment you can make. They wash easily, air-dry quickly, and wear well, so that you will not have to renew the investment each year. 'Polyprop', as it is affectionately called, is among a range of products which are designed to wick the moisture away from the body to avoid heat loss through evaporation. A long-sleeved polyprop shirt and tights will be the best base for winter running wear. Other textiles with wicking ability are available, and you can seek advice at your local running or outdoor camping store. Do not make the mistake of putting a cotton t-shirt on top of your polypropylene undershirt. The t-shirt, with its high absorbency, works like a sponge, and will be rapidly drenched with perspiration. It will then sit on top of you like a heat pump, pumping the heat *away* from your body. You should wear the polyprop with wind gear.

Gore-tex is another expensive fabric with protection properties. It feels like nylon, but has the unique ability to let the moisture from perspiration be evacuated towards the outside, but disallowing the penetration of moisture

(rain) from the outside. If you can afford it, and particularly if you live in a rugged climate zone, a goretex outer suit should complete your main outfit.

With a more restricted budget, you can still face the elements. What is most important with traditional fabrics is to be able to adapt your outerwear as you are running, to accommodate changing weather and running conditions. You mustn't be too warm, as you will perspire heavily, and then when heading back into the wind, you'll cool off too quickly.

Carry a wind jacket in a pouch, so that you can don it as needed. Wear several layers of clothing. For the top, start with thermal underwear,[8] followed by a wool sweater, and one or two (depending on the temperature) roomy sweat shirts. The layered approach allows you to trap warm air between the different garments, creating a kind of insulation. Be careful with comfortable cotton next to the skin, as it is absorbent as described above. A nylon wind-jacket will complete the top gear.

Woollen tights, two pairs of socks and sweat pants will do for the bottom. If it is snowy, rainy, or slushy, plastic bags on your feet, between the two layers of socks, will be particularly helpful.

Wear a woollen or polyprop cap to

---

8 I find that my bra is actually a great source of problems, even when wearing expensive polyprop. My bra will be soaked with perspiration, and I will get very cold, very quickly.

avoid losing heat from the head, and don't forget your gloves! Because the peripheral circulation clamps down in the cold, and particularly when you are running, when the larger muscles also require increased blood supply, your fingers will get very cold. You will often see competitive runners in important races with sleeveless jerseys, and gloves. Runners get cold fingers. I wear polyprop gloves (or cotton if it is not very cold), and will put heavy woollen mittens, or goretex shell mittens on top in very cold conditions. In some conditions, you will want to cover your face partially. A polyprop ski cap comes in handy on a bitter day.

Don't run too far away on a cold day. Make sure there is a way to cut things short if you need to. If it is windy, run into the wind to start your run, so that it can blow you back in. It can be quite a serious mistake to run with the wind at your back to start with, as you will get sweaty and warm, without realising how cold it truly is. On the way back, you'll be miserable! If a blizzard is raging, take a break, and wait until sunnier days. You can jump rope, go to the indoor pool, the gym, or just have an easy day to catch up on your reading.

Hot weather running

Heat can be a treacherous enemy! When your metabolic needs increase, as when you are running, your body becomes a mini-furnace. When making the extra energy for the running, heat is also produced. This heat needs to be dissipated to avoid overheating the body. There is a complex system of thermo-regulation which helps this extra heat to be eliminated by the body, and keep things cool. When the outside tempera-ture is very high, this is a difficult task, and a smart runner will know how to help the body out, and keep it from overheating.

Lots of elements affect your ability to stay cool. Of course, the outside tempera-ture is important. The hotter it is, the harder it will be to cool off. Other factors include the amount of wind (a hot, still day is a lot hotter than a hot, breezy day), the intensity of your running, your level of fitness, and the humidity level.

How does thermoregulation help you to stay cool? The excess heat is transported to the skin surface by blood flow. If the sweat glands perceive a high enough temperature, sweating takes place. The skin and the core temperature will go down as the sweat evaporates. Further cooling takes place by convection and conduction of heat from the skin towards the outside environment. When the outside temperature climbs, it becomes more difficult to transfer body temperature outward. Likewise, sweating becomes a less efficient way of cooling. If the atmospheric humidity climbs, the sweat cannot evaporate, because the air is already saturated in water.

Some people will be more susceptible to heat-related problems than others. Children are particularly prone. The ratio between body surface and mass is greater than in adults. A child produces more metabolic heat, but (s)he perspires less, acclimatises more slowly, and tends to drink less. Children should always be supervised when they perform sporting activities in hot weather, and they should be encouraged to drink amply. Other people who are at greater risk include:
- non-acclimatised runners
- minimally-trained runners (they produce less sweat)
- a runner with a cold, the flu, or a fever
- overweight runners
- runners with a history of bad heat tolerance
- old or very young runners
- runners with hangovers, who are likely to be dehydrated before they even start!

Overheating

The first signs of overheating are often very discreet. You might start perspiring very heavily, or you might stop perspiring altogether. You might feel a bit shivery, despite very high outside temperatures, or you could have a headache and nausea. These are all signs which should be taken seriously. At a more critical stage, you could be confused, and wobbly. At the 1984 Los Angeles Olympic marathon, the Swiss athlete Gabriele Andersen exhibited these signs as she entered the stadium, apparently unaware of where to go next. If the overheating continues, there can be seizures, cerebral oedema, coma and death. It pays to be careful!

Prevention

As always, the best treatment is prevention. You need to be aware of the risks, and how to avoid increasing them. If you are ill, and it is very hot, don't run! It is not worth it. When you go for a run on a hot day, wear lightweight, and light-coloured clothes. Wear a cap if the sun is bright. Acclimatise yourself progressively to the heat. Run a bit less to start with, and see if you can avoid the hottest hours of the day. Early morning or late evening runs may be the best way to handle the weather. When you are running, stay out of the sun when possible, choosing shady routes.

Drink as much fluid as you can, even if you are not thirsty. Thirst is actually a *late* sign of dehydration. In addition to staying well-hydrated during the day, you must drink during the run as well. A runner can lose anything from one to two litres of sweat an hour! When you get back from your run, drink several large glasses of water or sport replacement drinks. One way to tell if you are drinking enough is if you urinate frequently, and your urine is barely more than faintly tinted. Concentrated urine, and infrequent urination, would be sure signs of inadequate fluid intake.

When it is very hot, run with a

partner, or at least, let someone know where and for how long you are going to be running. You should make sure that there is some way of obtaining drinking water on your run. Being from Virginia, where it can get very hot in the summer, I love running in the heat. On very hot days, I run to the track, and make two-mile loops out and back. That way, every two miles I can take a drink from the hose, and rinse off. Don't go for a ten mile run in the country on a hot day if you aren't able to carry water with you.

It is also a good idea to wet your head before you run, because this will increase your ability to transfer heat outward. You can simply hose down, by sticking your head under the tap, or just dump a cup of water on your head.

If you sense that you have become overheated, despite these recommendations, you need to stop running, and cool down, by any means available. Get into the shade, and hose yourself all over. Wet your clothes, your head, and your entire body. You may actually need to apply ice packs to your arm pits and groin. Drink copiously, and seek medical attention if you don't feel better.

CHAPTER FIVE

A Woman's Body

MENSTRUAL IRREGULARITY

Women athletes, especially those who do endurance sports, may notice changes in their menstrual patterns. In some cases, a woman who trains regularly may notice that her cycles lengthen. Instead of regular 28-day cycles, she may go two, or even three months without menstruating, and without noticing any of the physiological changes she might have been aware of in the past associated with ovulation or the premenstrual period. The lengthening of menstrual cycle to greater than 35 days, but less than 90 is called oligomenorrhoea. Some women may cease menstruating altogether, or menstruate less than three to four times a year. This situation is called amenorrhoea. Some young girls who start participating in sport (notably running and ballet) prior to physiological maturation, may appear to postpone maturity by their exercise, and do not start to menstruate at the usual age. Of course, there are also many women (the majority), who will note no changes in their menstrual patterns, even though their training is intense and serious.

In the general population, at least 5% of women have long menstrual cycles, with rare, or no menstrual bleeding. In athletic women, as many as 20% may have these problems. The percentage is higher again in competitive, rather than recreational, athletes. There appear to be temporary, reversible changes in the delicate balance of oestrogen, progesterone, testosterone (and other hormones) in some women who run.

It might feel like a godsend, not to menstruate! I can remember looking forward to my first period as an affirmation of my fast-arriving adulthood. Some of my friends were already menstruating, and I felt a bit left out. And yet, it is sometimes uncomfortable. I usually feel very heavy and bloated during menstruation. Although it may feel better to skip those periods, there can be some serious long-term consequences to not having any.

If you are not having periods, it makes sense to see a gynaecologist and talk it over. There can be reasons not related to running for ceasing menstruation or it may be that the increased exercise is the culprit. Either way, steps may still need to be taken.

Bone density and running

Remember, when great-aunt Jane fell and broke her femur? They said she had osteoporosis. What that meant is that the fall didn't break her hip, she had a *spontaneous* fracture (it just snapped, it was so brittle), and that made her fall.

An accidental, and yet very important discovery was made several years ago, when a very fit woman runner, who had ceased menstruating, had a bone scan. The physician who looked at the result was astounded to note that this very active young woman had a wrist bone resembling that of a post-menopausal woman, with similar lack of bone calcification. Weight-bearing exercise had always been propounded as an excellent means for ensuring optimum bone density. Further studies have shown that inadequate bone density may be the price to pay for absent menstrual periods. How does this work?

It is well known that if the ovaries are removed from a woman for medical reasons she will be at high risk for reduced bone density. This is because the ovaries secrete oestrogen, which is important in the calcification process. These women usually take hormone replacement therapy to avoid such complications as osteoporosis. In a woman who does not menstruate because of athletic activities, at least two things may be taking place. Either, unusually, she does not bleed, but otherwise maintains a normal hormonal cycle, with ovulation, and normal hormone levels; or, she does not bleed, nor does she have normal ovulation. If she doesn't ovulate, she may fail to produce adequate hormones such as oestrogen or progesterone, and she may develop weak bones. After a certain amount of lost bone density, these women become increasingly at risk of fractures, either stress fractures related to their running, or later in life. Furthermore, not ovulating affects a woman's ability to conceive a child, though this is usually totally reversible with proper management.

So, should a woman who stops menstruating when she runs, stop running? Absolutely not! Running is very good for all of the body systems. The absence of exercise is not *better* for bone density, and sedentariness is known to have terrible side-effects for the cardio-vascular system. There are many ways to manage exercise related menstrual irregularity, but in order to do so, it is important to understand a bit more about the underlying reasons for its existence.

Reasons for menstrual irregularity in exercising women

The answers are not totally clear yet, because the study of menstrual irregularity in exercising women is a new one. At present, a few factors have been positively related to the cessation, or lengthening of cycles in women runners.

• Excessive thinness or weight loss

In severely malnourished women, such as anorexics, who have had very significant weight loss, menstrual periods cease. It is thought that there might be a similar relationship between the low weight (low body fat) of a highly trained runner, and the athletic amenorrhoea. Fatty tissues produce oestrogen, and perhaps the loss of body fat is sufficient to lower the oestrogen levels beyond that which is necessary to sustain menstruation. Some studies have pointed out that women who lost more than 10 pounds when they started running are at higher risk than those who did not lose weight. Similarly,

women weighing less than 8 stone 4 lb are also more frequently concerned. On the other hand, many very lean women have normal cycles and some runners with much higher body fat may be amenorrhoeic! Confusing, no?

Also related to low body fat is dieting. A surprising number of very lean and fit female runners continue to watch what they eat very closely, even though they do not have eating disorders. Some runners, even very good ones, tend to use the scale as an indicator of fitness, instead of the stopwatch, seeing any fluctuation in weight as an indication of declining competitive preparedness. Women with menstrual irregularities are indeed more likely to fall in this category of under-eaters.

• Exercise intensity

Women who run fast, or a lot, are more likely to have menstrual irregularity. There is more amenorrhoea in women who train more than 50 miles per week. Of course, it is not easy to separate high mileage from low body fat, competition and related high stress. Women who train that much usually race, and the stress related to competition and high training load may impact the cycle significantly.

• Number of children

Women who have never had children are more frequently amenorrhoeic than those who have.

• Stress levels

Women who run excessively, who rarely rest, who feel an absolute need to run, and who can't do without it ('hooked' to running), who tend to be depressed, or extremely rigid with themselves, and finally, who seem to be particularly preoccupied with food or weight, are more likely to have menstrual irregularity.

• Age

Women who matured late are more likely to have menstrual irregularities than women who had their first period early.

Management of menstrual irregularities

It is important to consult a health-care professional who understands the problems of the female athlete in order to obtain adequate guidance for this problem. The current state of research is that we are learning more and more about these problems, and only a keen and interested person will be likely to be up to date on the most current recommendations. It is quite likely that the following information would need to be covered with the doctor:

1. Is there a chance that you have been overtraining, and can we look at the indicators which would confirm this?
   - has there been a decline in your performance?
   - have you felt fatigued, heavy-legged, sluggish?
   - is there an increase in your resting heart rate?
   - are you more irritable than usual?

RECIPE FOR OPTIMUM BONE STRENGTH

- Don't smoke.

- Make sure your calcium intake is adequate (4 to 5 portions a day of calcium rich products – see chapter six), or take supplements as advised by your physician.

- Discuss Vitamin D supplementation with your physician.

- Get adequate fresh air and sunshine to enable the assimilation of Vitamin D.

- Continue weight-bearing exercise (running), but do not be excessive about the amount you run (see previous page).

- Consider hormone replacememt when appropriate, and as directed by your physician.

– do you feel you have lost enthusiasm, joy, and/or libido?

2. Is your dietary intake adequate? (A minimum 3-day dietary record and evaluation is desirable.)
   – have you had any recent changes in appetite?
   – are you, or have you been on a diet?
   – have you lost weight?

3. Do you feel happy with your current health status?
   – your body weight?
   – your body shape?

4. What is your current progesterone/oestrogen status? (Blood tests will determine this.)

With answers to these questions, your doctor may make recommendations about either your training, your diet, the possibility of hormone replacement therapy, or all three. In most cases, it will not be difficult to set things straight. He or she may ask for a bone scan to look at your skeleton and evaluate the effect any menstrual irregularity may already have had on your bone density. The absence of abnormal findings on the scan should not lead you into a false sense of security. The purpose of treatment for menstrual irregularity is mainly to protect you as you go down the road, not just to fix what may already be amiss. It remains important, however, for all active women to optimise their bone density in order to ensure a long and healthy existence.

RUNNING AND PMT

Many women are uncomfortable in the days leading up to their menstrual periods. Complaints can range from swollen and tender breasts to mood swings, abdominal discomfort, sleep disturbance, anxiety, fluid retention and constipation (to name a few). As running can affect menstrual cycle, it is not outrageous to consider whether or not running can change any of these symptoms. Studies have shown that undertaking a running exercise programme can help to decrease overall premenstrual symptoms, specifically those related to breast tenderness and fluid retention.[9] So, even if you don't feel particularly well, it is probably a good idea to maintain some degree of exercise during that period.

If your breasts are tender, make sure to have a good sport bra so that you are not uncomfortable when running. I suggest that you run easily at a relaxed pace so as not to exaggerate any feelings of stress you might have. I tend to get

---

9 Prior *et al.*, Exercise decreases premenstrual symptoms, *Fertility and Sterility*, 1987, p402–408.

irritable during that phase of my cycle. I get mad at my speed sessions, and aggravated. I usually feel happier if I simply postpone such sessions until I am in a better frame of mind.

Studies have also been done to investigate the influence of the different phases of the menstrual cycle on performance, and there has been little evidence to show that there is a correlation. Women have won Olympic medals while menstruating, pre-menstrual, post-menstrual, ovulatory – in short, in all phases of the menstrual cycle. Many women will report that they feel better in one phase or another. Someone with marked pre-menstrual water retention or weight gain may feel less comfortable exercising, while others would dread exercising while menstruating.

To sum up, the different phases of the menstrual cycle, including the pre-menstrual phase, may have an effect on how you feel. Effects of the menstrual cycle on athletic performance vary from woman to woman, and it has no effect at all for many. Negative symptoms during the pre-menstrual period may actually be alleviated by exercise.

Heather D.

My running time is more important to me now that I have two children. It is my sanity break. It's a little bit of space for me. I feel better and that benefits my children.

PREGNANCY AND RUNNING

Pregnancy used to be a time during which mothers-to-be were advised to restrict all physical activity. Today, we are much more aware of what a pregnant woman can, and cannot, do safely. Pregnant women are advised to continue with a normal lifestyle whenever possible. Can pregnant women run? Does running put the unborn child or its mother at risk in any way? What measures can be taken to make running safer for a pregnant woman?

I have had two children. Both were born in excellent health, despite the fact that I ran up until the last days of pregnancy in both cases. Ingrid Kristiansen (world marathon record holder), Joan Benoit (gold medalist in the first women's Olympic marathon), Mary Decker (double world champion in middle distance track events) and Liz McColgan (among the world leaders for all distances above 5000 metres during her running career), all ran during their pregnancies and suffered no ill-consequences for themselves or their children. However, not all women can run during pregnancy. There are some cases where that would be excessively dangerous. In all cases, precautions must be taken to ensure that the pregnancy is safe and happy.

There will be many changes in the pregnant woman's body. Her blood volume will increase by 40%, and her cardiac output by 30 to 50%. As a result, the resting heart rate of the mother-to-be will be much higher than usual during the pregnancy. Exercise which may have seemed like child's play prior to pregnancy (e.g.; climbing the stairs, or walking to the bus stop) may leave her winded. Oxygen consumption increases during pregnancy, but it is the uterus and the foetus which are the beneficiaries, not the mother! In fact, she will have less than usual. What is more, the uterus will push into the abdominal cavity, and restrict the movement of the diaphragm, which increases the feelings of breathlessness she may already have.

Her centre of gravity shifts as well, and she may have problems with balance. It becomes easy to fall, even when doing activities much gentler than running.

To sum up: running is difficult during pregnancy, but in many cases it is still possible to run.

Let us see how.

Set your goals

As in all things, goal setting will enhance the chances for success. Running during pregnancy should be undertaken to:

– have some time to relax and do what you enjoy in a very low-key environment
– maintain the habitual nature of your training
– maintain minimal cardio-vascular and neuromuscular fitness

It would be dangerous to have a goal of keeping your weight down, or of improving your performance during

---

ADVICE FOR A PREGNANT RUNNER

- Medical advice must be sought, and followed, if you wish to run during pregnancy.
- Be familiar with the list of 'don't run signs' (see later this chapter).
- Wear comfortable loose clothing, (oversized boxer shorts, loose tights).
- Wear shoes with stable, wide soles to improve your balance.
- Run on smooth, soft surfaces.
- Only run gently, and keep your heart rate within the target zone. This may take slowing down your pace to a mere crawl!
- Eat adequately, and drink plenty of fluids. Take pre-natal vitamins if prescribed by your doctor or midwife.
- Be even more careful when the weather is hot, and avoid overheating and dehydration.

actually improved in a group of women after childbirth, as compared to a control group. So, even if you are unable to exercise during pregnancy, you have every chance once you get back to your baseline training of being at least as fit, if not fitter, than prior to conceiving.

Reduce the quantity and quality of your training

Since twenty minutes to a half hour of aerobic activity, three times a week, is the minimum recommended to ensure cardio-vascular fitness, such would be enough for a pregnant woman who wishes to continue running, even if she is a competitive runner. During the first trimester of pregnancy, however, fatigue and morning sickness can be enough to dissuade you from running even as little as that. If, on the other hand, you are feeling well enough, you may continue to run, reducing your mileage only slightly, or not at all.

You will probably notice that you

pregnancy. Any woman who discovers that she is secretly trying to do either of these things during pregnancy would do well to take a break from running, in order to protect herself and her baby from the excesses to which this could lead. Women who are hard on themselves, or have trouble holding back, should stop running during their pregnancy. Running during pregnancy is not without risks, and it is only advisable when the mother-to-be is truly in control of her desire to run. Stopping for nine months will not erase all the benefits already acquired; you can switch to easier forms of exercise and starting back is not as hard as you might think.

Furthermore, some research has shown that there are athletic training benefits to pregnancy, all by itself! Physiological gauges of performance

The rule of thumb for running during pregnancy

- Easy runs only.
- Hydrate yourself well.
- Avoid running in the heat.
- Do not run on rough surfaces.

need to urinate frequently in the early months of pregnancy. This is because, as the uterus takes up more space in the pelvis to accommodate the growing foetus, it applies pressure on the bladder. It is a good idea to make sure there is at least one place (and probably more!) on your running course where you can use a toilet. You may also be at risk for urinary tract infections throughout pregnancy. It is important to keep up good fluid intake to reduce that risk (which is high in chronically dehydrated runners, who **never** drink enough anyway!), and you should consult your physician if you have any burning or discomfort when you urinate.

Throughout pregnancy, you must be closely aware of the potential danger signals, must stop all athletic activity if they appear, and seek medical advice promptly.

The second trimester often brings relief from morning sickness and everything starts feeling better. The uterus moves out, into the abdominal cavity, and pressure on the bladder is somewhat relieved. Since pregnancy starts to 'show', everyone takes very good care of you, and you feel great! You can keep on running, or resume, if you had stopped during the earlier months. Run according to how you feel, avoiding any work-outs which make your heart rate or body temperature climb excessively. You should just be going for gentle jogs.

You've got no racing goals in sight anyway, so speed work, tempo running and hill work is not necessary. You will sharpen back up again after childbirth, and right now, you should focus only on the goals mentioned above: keeping up a good habit, and maintaining minimal cardio-vascular fitness.

You should also be wary of running over uneven terrain; with a changed centre of gravity, you could fall, and hurt yourself or your baby. As your body prepares for childbirth, your ligaments gain flexibility, which can actually lead to strain. They don't stabilise as well as they did before pregnancy. Avoid any quick changes of direction when you run, or over-vigorous stretching. Regularly discuss your exercise programme with

---

DON'T RUN, AND CONTACT YOUR DOCTOR OR MIDWIFE IF:

- You have vaginal bleeding, no matter how little.
- You have contractions.
- You have a fever.
- You notice that the baby has stopped moving, or is moving less.
- You are fatigued.
- Your ears are ringing, or you are dizzy.
- You have a headache.
- Your heart feels like it is 'racing', or 'skipping beats'.
- You have a sudden, noticeable increase in weight.
- You have oedema in your feet, your face, or elsewhere.

your physician, and the way you feel before, during and after your runs. You should not plan on running races for competitive purposes during pregnancy.

In the third trimester, running gets a good deal more difficult. With twenty-two extra pounds, a diaphragm which is crammed into too small a space, and a heart which is racing away, even at rest, you need to cut way back! Make sure you are not running any faster than 'talking' pace. It will be the best gauge of exertion. If you can't run and talk, don't run! Many women find swimming to be a very satisfactory substitute. The water gently supports the body, and there is less of a risk of overheating or trauma. I found that running was still possible, but only at a snail's pace, and for about fifteen to twenty minutes at a time. Any more than that seemed impossible! I only ran every other day at the most, and it didn't keep me from coming back, fitter than a fiddle, within months of childbirth.

Childbirth

The athletic training of a runner is excellent preparation for childbirth. Many of the visual imagery, breathing, and control exercises are closely related to what we do to prepare us for competition. The conditioning advantages of training are beneficial, should labour be drawn-out. In all cases the runner

can approach childbirth confident that she is strong, fit and well-prepared: a bonus for both herself, and her child.

POST NATAL COMEBACK – Better than ever!

Each woman adapts to motherhood in her own manner. Recovery time will be a very individualised thing. You need to make sure that you have given your body enough time to rest before you start back again. The issues to take into consideration are: problems encountered during pregnancy, the length or difficulty of labour, Caesarian section, episiotomy, blood loss, infant health, number of children at home, availability of domestic help, and so on.

A minimum of one month off after a normal vaginal delivery of a healthy

---

Heather D.
(27, after the birth of her second child)

It was incredibly hard when I started running after my baby was born. The first time I went out, I ran down a hill and around the playing fields. I couldn't do more than six minutes before I had to walk! I was so tired! However I was persistent and went out every day, but I went really slowly at first. I talked to myself and said, 'Just go at a snail's pace.' I started feeling better very quickly. My breathing improved, and things felt easier. I slowly built my speed back up, and in about two to three weeks, I could run for a full half hour.

infant to a couple where grandma is available to help out at home is required. After a Caesarian section, two months are *de rigeur*, and the surgeon's green light is required. Certainly, you will read stories about women who were back to racing within two weeks of delivery, but imitating such stories leads to imprudence. There is no hurry to get back into shape, so why take such risks? Many women find that they will become better runners after they have borne children. I was able to set personal records over many distances within a few months of the births of both of my children. On the other hand, that sweet little bundle of joy is going to interrupt your sleep at night, and demand your attention all day, creating a physically stressful situation to which you owe your tired body the time to adapt. It also takes some energy to learn how to be a mother, even if you are just refreshing your memory.

When can I run again?

You can and should walk, as soon as you feel able. This helps to avoid the risk of phlebitis, or inflammation of the veins which is common in post-partum mothers. Walking up and down the halls of the maternity wing is a good opportunity to start – the earlier, the better.

You are not going to look or feel as you did prior to pregnancy the moment the baby is born. I was very disappointed not to be able to fit into the new dress my mother bought me to go home in, even though I had not put on excess pounds during pregnancy. You will be in a hurry to feel 'like before', and to start galloping along forest paths. Getting back in shape may feel like a monstrous task, but looking back on it later, you will be surprised at how easy it actually was.

Keep up the walking. With my first baby, walking more than 50 yards was a chore, whereas with my second, I could walk miles with ease within days. I don't mean to suggest that first babies are harder to recover from; rather that you won't recover the same way, or at the same speed, each time. Walk around the block as soon as you feel strong enough, but make sure that the walking doesn't tire you out too much.

When can you go back to running? My advice would be to wait until you feel perfectly ready to start back again, and then add on an additional two weeks. I do sound like a meanie, don't I? Well, you have to be cautious, or you risk getting into trouble with complications or ill health. Many a mother will look back on the months following childbirth and remember more upper respiratory infections (colds and the like) than usual, or other little health problems which were probably due to the extreme strain that pregnancy and motherhood put on her body. Waiting a few weeks longer may, in fact, make it easier for you to stay healthy.

Your first run

The first time you run, fifteen minutes will be long enough, no matter how fit you were prior to pregnancy. Run very slowly, on a soft surface. The purpose of this run is a quick check on the machinery to make sure that everything is primed and ready for running.

Increase your running time by five to ten minutes per run. Don't be disappointed that your body doesn't feel very responsive. It will take remarkably less time than you may have thought to get back into shape, but it won't happen instantly.

The second week of running, don't increase the distance too much, but add in an additional run or two. You will need moral support at this point, because, if you are like me, you will be feeling a bit like a whale out of water, or a snail in sneakers! Hang in there, because things are going to get better very soon.

If all continues to go well, try some quality work the third week. In the middle of one of your runs, throw in a three-minute burst, recover for two, and repeat two to three times. Or, if you prefer, do some 30/30 for a total of five minutes or slightly more. For the next month, progressively start introducing such work-outs, and increasing the duration of each. At the end of that month, you may add a long run.

You can start thinking about competing over distances less than ten kilometres after a month of this regime. Your preliminary results in racing shoes may not be quite up to par, but again, it won't take long. Stick with it! Many women find they are able to run much better times after they have had children. There is no known explanation for this. Scientists are studying the question. Might there be a maturation of hormones due to pregnancy which would explain this? Or does the cardio-vascular burden of pregnancy contribute to fitness in a way that long distance training cannot? I have a purely anecdotal hypothesis. I was fortunate enough to make significant progress in my times after the birth of my first child. I knocked 22 seconds off my 3000 metre track time, without feeling I was working any harder. The same thing happened when my daughter was born five years later. I thought that any benefit I might have gained from the first pregnancy was a one-shot deal. But, six months after Mélanie, my second, was born, I knocked a big minute off my ten kilometre time! When I read back over my training logs, one thing is quite apparent. With the birth of each child, I became less and less in control of my day. My training had to fit in when and where it could: between work, children's school, my husband's run, getting dinner on the table... I had to follow a rigid schedule which was more restrictive, but in a sense, more organised. To this day I can't just pick up and go whenever I feel like it, but on the other hand, it would be unlikely I would skip a run as I might have in the past. I need a little bit of time, just for me, far away from the house and the 'mummy!'s This means that running has taken a more important spot in my life than before, and maybe my increased commitment has improved my performance.

Until the scientists are able to tell us the true reasons behind this phenomenon, we will just look at the Kristiansens, and Decker-Slaneys, and take heart in their own improvements after childbirth.

Breast feeding

Breast feeding is an excellent solution for both mum and baby. From the standpoint of a running mum, think of the advantages! No bottles to wash, no formula to prepare! It also saves money. For baby, the advantages are enormous, as mother's milk is what is best suited to baby's health and growth. Furthermore, lactation stimulates the secretion of hormones which facilitate mum's recovery. Breast feeding mothers will find that their uterus goes back to its usual size much more quickly than mothers who do not breast feed their babies. Lactation will not wear you out. Often, the fatigue of pregnancy and delivery is attributed to breast feeding, when that is truly not the case. If you get enough rest, and eat properly, there should be no problem. I have spent almost three years of my life breast feeding my children. I continued training and racing during this period, and even set personal records! It made my life so much easier to breast feed. I could go on road trips without having to worry about bottles spoiling en route.

From a practical standpoint, the nursing mother should try to run after feeding baby, because chances for engorgement seem greater after a run. And of course, proper breast support is vital.

Avoiding engorgement

- Run after feeding baby.
- Wear a supportive bra.
- Drink three or more litres of fluid a day.
- If breasts are painful, continue nursing, but apply warm compresses, and contact your local La Leche League or midwife for advice.

Weight loss

It is unusual to lose all the weight gained during pregnancy right away. The baby and the placenta are only 40% of the total weight gain, in most cases. That means that when you start running again you will undoubtedly be carrying some extra kilos, which reduce your performance ability. Fat weight is less well vascularised than muscle weight, so its oxygenation capacity is less. You should not jump on a diet right away, because your nutritional requirements are high at this time. If you can whittle away a pound a week, you will be doing fine!

Urinary incontinence

Some women may find that they are incontinent of urine when they start running again. This is due to weakness of the urinary sphincter, or trauma to the bladder during delivery.

You can improve this problem with special exercises. When you use the toilet, and are urinating, deliberately stop the flow of urine, and hold that contraction for a moment or two. Repeat the exercise several times during the day. Once you are able to do that easily, try to contract the same muscles when you are not urinating. You can do that at any time, and no one will know you are practising! Do talk to your doctor as well. Additional measures

may be necessary. It is unlikely that you will need to stop running. Always urinate before you go running, and empty your bladder regularly during your run. It may take some time to fix things up, but running is not the culprit in this case.

Go Mummy!

Nothing is more important to a child than their mother. Your children may need you day and/or night, and it is the one responsibility that there is no way to get out of. It often feels like we have no control any more. Once you get everything organised and ready to go, the car breaks down, the babysitter gets sick, or your youngest child falls off a wall and breaks her arm! Often, taking care of your children makes you forget to take care of yourself. It would be a shame to stop running because of the kids. It shouldn't be necessary to do so. It is possible to balance the lot.

There are some times that control and organisation is possible, and planning ahead will often make them work more smoothly. If you are in paid employment, which days are there more staff at work, and might you be able to take a long lunch break? If you're at home with the kids, when does your husband finish early and might he look after them while you run? Which days can you get a babysitter?

The biggest issues for the running mum are 'When am I free?' and 'When can I get child care?' You need to be innovative about when you run. You may need to get up early in the morning, and run before they are awake, or wait until they have gone to bed, and run in the evening. These solutions may involve running in the dark, which should prompt you to look for some partners, or an established group of morning or evening runners. This also may require you to reduce the amount of time you are running. If you run regularly, there will be no long-term effect on your running, if you run 20 minutes instead of 30, or 30 instead of 45. If you must reduce your running

time due to this kind of scheduling, do try to stick in at least one longer run every week, on the weekend, for example.

You may also wish to explore innovative child care options. If you have other friends who run, look for a co-operative arrangement. If each mother gives up one run a week to look after the children, you may all have your week-day runs covered! Maybe one of the high school students in your neighbourhood would like some work: especially if it's only for a half-an-hour at a time.

Consider bringing your children to the track for a run. When my oldest was still in a stroller, he would come on a sunny day, and sit all bundled up while I ran around the track. I could see him from all vantage points, and could run (though on a distinctly uninteresting course). As the children get older, they can play at the track, once they have learnt track etiquette and safety. They should not cross the track in front of runners, should not be allowed on the infield if throwers or field event athletes are training, and should be kept away from the steeplechase pit (filled with water). All of the tracks on which I have trained have had grassy areas where the children enjoyed playing, and so they would often come along. Once again, I could see them from all points on my run.

Of course, baby strollers are now being designed to allow mothers or fathers to train while pushing their children in front of them. These are wonderful, though expensive, appliances which fit children of all sizes. If you choose to purchase a runner's stroller, make sure your children are adequately dressed when you go out for your run/push. You will be much warmer than they are due to the energy created by your exercise. They will be quite exposed, and not as active. Dress them accordingly.

Once the children are old enough to go to school, running times are best assigned to those hours if possible. If you live in an urban centre, and work-out at a gym, advocate a play group, or child care provision if they don't have it already, so that you can leave your younger children there while you go for your run.

It becomes more difficult to run with your spouse once you have children. He may or may not have been your most regular partner, but he should also be your best babysitter.

If you both like to run at a given park, one of you should run there, and do your work-out. The other can come with the children, make a quick switch, and do their own work-out with a run home at the end. The one who trained first has had time to get home, and put dinner on the stove. It takes some juggling! Running partners may end up with unconventional schedules and late dinners.

It may sometimes be very difficult to organise your running when you have children. You mustn't give in just because it is hard. It is an important part of your life which you shouldn't sacrifice. You are teaching an important lesson to your children through your own physical activity.

They will learn young that physical fitness is a part of personal health and well-being. They will also learn to adjust their lives to a healthy lifestyle. You may find that you will have to opt for quality rather than quantity while your children are young. You may have to lower the amount of mileage you are doing, because of time constraints. You can use that opportunity to throw in some quality work-outs that you might not have thought about doing otherwise. When child care is unavailable, or one of your children is ill, you may opt for home work-outs. Buy a jump rope, do some stretching, or if you have the financial resources, purchase a stationary bicycle, or a high-quality treadmill.

Some days, it will not be possible to run at all. It's not the end of the world, and you will not lose all the fitness you have acquired. It is not too difficult to return to your top level, regardless of your age, as long as you maintain a minimal level of fitness. Don't give it up, just keep going. You will be glad you did. So will your children.

RUNNING AFTER MENOPAUSE
– There's no reason to stop!

The golden years

Do we really slow down when we get older, or do we get older because we slow down? It is a tricky question. My mother has always had a list of things that you have to get done by a certain age, or you are 'too old' to do them any more. ('That woman is too old to have hair so long', or 'don't you think you are too old to wear dresses that short?'). How many limitations have we placed on ourselves that we think are attributable to age, but in fact are simply due to the fact that we have denied them to ourselves by preconceived ideas about what is appropriate to our age? It often begins when we leave school or university, and enter the work-force. We don't make the time to keep exercising, and suddenly it becomes hard to run to catch the bus. Not because we are a few years older, but because we are a few more years away from the healthy, active people that we were all born to be!

Sport, and running in particular, can be a very helpful tool for the assimilation of the physiological changes which take place in older women. The words of Francoise Lamothe, who continues, at age 72 (1995) to pound the pavement, mile after mile, is an excellent illustration of what running can offer the mature woman.

Thank you, o running, for giving us the feeling that, despite menopause, we still exist: from the moment we decide to trot down the alleyways in colourful tights with a number pinned to our fronts. This awareness of still being a part of things, and of still belonging to the family of young people of all ages who love their bodies, and who use them, is a marvellous source of balance, of confidence in self and in others, in life and in longevity...

Menopause marks the end of the biologically fertile period in the life of a woman. The impact of hormonal changes varies from one woman to another. With the decrease in oestrogen secretion, the arteries become less elastic, and women become more prone to cardio-vascular disorders. They lose the advantage they had over their male counterparts, who in earlier years were more susceptible to such afflictions. Osteoporosis, or insufficient bone density, may result from the lower oestrogen levels. Many women have difficulty adjusting to such changes, both physically and psychologically.

Edith M. (72)

When I was younger, a woman's place was thought to be in the home: to clean, to dust, and bake, and all those things. I have been running since I was 59. It gives me a real high! I enjoy it so much! I am always looking for a fresh challenge, and enjoy being outdoors. I just like it.

Well, it is a good thing we have running! For all these problems, running can supply a convenient and efficient remedy.

Running enhances the cardio-vascular potential, and increases the diameter of major arteries. What an excellent way to counter the hormonally induced changes to the cardio-vascular system! Bone density is enhanced by weight-bearing exercise. Not only should women of all ages be undertaking such activities as an investment in future bone strength, older women can still benefit greatly from running and other forms of bone-strengthening exercise. It is certainly not too late! Running can also help to bridge the emotionally difficult times when an older women may feel down. There are many changes in her body, as well as her lifestyle. Her children may have flown the coop, and her home-based activities may have changed dramatically. Many women find, once their children are out on their own, that they had not set any personal goals beyond that of their children, and there may be a terrible feeling of emptiness. Once again, Françoise Lamothe offers great words of wisdom:

Thanks to the use of my legs and my lungs, so unfortunately ignored by me before,[10] not only my body has become lighter, so have my spirits! In the stride, the vision of all things has become more simple, more natural and more pleasant. Optimism shines through the astonishment of discovering the previously mysterious workings of my own body!

To be in good health after age 40, 50 or even 80 is what we hope for. As

> Françoise Lamothe (71)
>
> I believe that running, in the life of a woman, regardless of her social background, is much more than a pleasant pastime. It is a vital part of life, not only for her health, but for her sense of accomplishment.

healthy sportswomen, we do much more than hope for health. We are active participants in the quest for well-being. Many over-40 runners are people who have run since their childhood. Others are those who have hit a mid-life crisis, and in a moment of panic, or of 'mortality consciousness' have decided to put away the cigarettes, and regain a physical participation in life. You realise, more than ever, that you won't get a second chance, and you try to stack the cards in your favour. Not a bad idea! Running is a good way to start. You are likely to find other women eager to give it a try.

Age is not a deterrent to performance. Joyce Smith, aged 43, a British runner, could run the 26 miles of the marathon in 2h 29, at a time when only four women in the world had ever run faster! Lorraine Moller, from New Zealand, finished third in the Olympic marathon at Barcelona at age 37. Miki Gorman won the New York marathon in 1976 at the age of 41 years, and Sister Marion Irvine of California qualified for the American Olympic trials with a time of

---

10 Françoise didn't start running until age 55!

OESTROGEN, CALCIUM, EXERCISE AND BONES

Oestrogen contributes to the fixation of calcium in bones and what gives bones their density and strength. After menopause, bones lose some of their mineral content. It is important, therefore, to consider the best ways to optimise bone density after menopause, and to discuss the best strategy with your physician.

Oestrogen

If you have no contra-indications to taking oestrogen, your physician may advise you to take supplements early on. Bone demineralisation is very rapid in the first years of hormonal changes. However, oestrogen is not suitable for everyone, especially if there is a personal or family history of breast cancer.

Calcium

After menopause, calcium requirements will increase. You need 1500 mg of calcium per day. This can be achieved through your diet or supplementation.

Physical Activity

The beneficial effects of weight-bearing activities are well established, and are vital to the good health of post-menopausal women.

2h 52 for the marathon at the age of 55!

Certainly these women are not typical run-of-the-mill fitness runners. They show, however, that age need not be an obstacle to high-level performance. Therefore it needn't be a hindrance for simple fitness activities either. The late George Sheehan, inspirational runner, writer, speaker and physician, would often use the excellent example of Eula Weaver. At age 80, her physician told her that if she did not start an exercise rehabilitation programme, she would probably be bedridden as a result of cardio-vascular degeneration. Instead of sighing, and handing herself over to the ravages of age, she chose to get on the ball. She started walking, and later running. At over 90 years of age, she was still running a mile a day, as well as pedalling away on her exercise bike. It is never too late (or too soon!) to take responsibility for your own health.

How to start?

First and foremost, medical advice must be sought for any person who plans to undertake an exercise programme for the first time after the age of 40. This is especially true if you are overweight, have a personal or family history of heart disease or asthma, or if you have lived the high life for many years (moderate or greater use of cigarettes, alcohol or drugs of any kind). This is sometimes the hardest step. It is downright painful to have to receive a lecture from a health professional: 'You really should be doing something about your life!', or, if you are basically already healthy, 'Why don't you do something more suited to your age?' That is why it is important to approach this consultation with your physician in a well thought-out manner. What do you want to obtain from the doctor?

1. A thorough physical examination, including ECG, to detect any potential risk factors to exercise at this time.

2. Guidance about what other modification to your lifestyle would be in order.

3. Active support for the fitness prog-ramme you are about to undertake.

If you are not given the go-ahead, or your physician is not supportive, seek a second opinion. This is not a suggestion that you 'doctor-shop' until you can find someone who will tell you what you want to hear, but rather, a safety check to make sure that your doctor's personal bias does not interfere with his/her professional advice.

Remember, cardiac bypass patients are encouraged and guided in their exercise rehabilitation, so there can truly be few cases where exercise would be contra-indicated. There is no conclusive scientific evidence to support the idea that running can cause osteo-arthritis in normal joints. One study of runners over the age of 70 showed that the incidence of arthritis in the runners was not higher than in a matched group of non-runners.[11] The same author believes, and has shown through his research, that running appears to help preserve musculoskeletal function in older people. If your doctor is one of those 'Crazy runners! Look what it did to Jim Fixx!' kind of people, you will probably need to look for another doctor.

The older woman who starts running for the first time can follow the same recommendations which are outlined for the true beginner. It may take a bit longer to get in the groove, and this is where it is important to remember to avoid comparing yourself to anyone other than yourself. If the programme I have outlined seems to move forward too quickly, that is not a sign that you are too old, rather an indication that it will take a bit more time. Although adolescence is the best time to improve your capacity to run, the approach as a mature sportswoman is not to make a better machine so much as it is to get the best you can out of the machine you've got. We generally use such a small portion of our potential that it is a surprise to realise just how much we can do!

---

11 Lane, N. E and colleagues. *Aging, long distance running and the development of musculoskeletal disability: A controlled study.* Journal of the American Medical Association 255,5 1147–1151.

CHAPTER SIX

A Woman Runner's Guide to Good Eating

It is not the purpose of this book to give you basic dietary recommendations. There are many excellent books on the market that address the basic nutritional needs of active adults.[12] There are special considerations that a runner must take into account, and there are even more specific issues affecting the female runner. Those are the concerns to which this chapter is devoted. The healthier the diet, the better it is for a woman runner, so we cannot totally ignore the discussion of balanced diet. I'll try to keep that to a minimum, so we can fully explore the aspects of diet which are different, or simply, more important, to a dedicated runner.

GETTING YOUR FILL
Adequate Nutrition for a Woman Runner

What makes a runner's nutritional requirements different from those of a

12 See 'Recommended Reading'

non-runner? Most obviously, perhaps, is the fact that it takes energy to run, and dietary energy intake must be adequate. Secondly, a runner will have restorative needs. Not only must energy stores be replenished after their depletion during exercise, but muscle mass and bone density must be maintained, and that requires the sufficient supply of building materials for construction and reconstruction. For all the metabolic exchanges to take place, and to allow the transport and elimination of waste, there must also be ample hydration.

CARBOHYDRATES
– fuel to burn

Carbohydrates are the main energy source for running. They are principally found in fruits and vegetables, starches and sugars. They are stored in the muscles and the liver in a form called 'glycogen', and can be mobilised from these sites, as needed. To be properly prepared for running, you must eat a sufficient amount and the suitable type of carbohydrates to create ample glycogen stores.

Carbohydrates take many forms

Simple sugars and starches are the energetic forms of carbohydrates. Cellulose is also a carbohydrate, but cannot be used for fuel in humans.[13] These terms refer to the chemical construction of the carbohydrate molecule. The simple sugars are in a very simple form, and cannot be broken down into a smaller sugar particle.

Complex carbohydrates, including starches, on the other hand, are made up of simple sugars bonded together to create more complex compounds. The bond must be broken down before the simple sugars can be used. Complex carbohydrates are generally metabolised more slowly than simple sugars. But there are some complex carbohydrates which are metabolised as quickly (if not more so) than their simple cousins. Knowing this can be helpful when you choose your pre-training, or pre-race diet.

If you don't eat enough carbohydrates

with quick metabolic entry, you will be sluggish when you fire up the engines (when you start an activity). On the other hand, these start-up sugars are as rapidly consumed as they are metabolised. If there are enough slow carbohydrates, there is a steady release of energy and the slow carbohydrates will pick up where the others left off, supplying a regular influx of glucose to fuel the muscle contractions. If you are low on slow carbohydrates, you'll be in quite a bad way. You will not have the fuel necessary to continue exercising, and your blood sugar level will plummet, leaving you hypoglycaemic. If you eat more carbohydrates than you need, your body will store them, but as fat, a less available energy reserve.

Choosing carbohydrates – which forms do I need?

So, how do you know which carbohydrates to eat? You can find out by trial and by error, of course. What makes you feel good? What makes you feel drained, and low on energy? Or, you can take a look at the glycaemic index (Figure 22), and apply the information it contains. The glycaemic index is a sort of scale. It rates common foods based on their impact on the blood sugar level. Foods which raise your blood sugar level quickly are higher on the list than those which

---

13 Even though not energy producing, cellulose has a role in the digestive process and should be included in the well-balanced diet. It provides the body with dietary fibre which is necessary for healthy bowel function.

elevate your blood sugar more gradually. Some foods, despite being carbohydrates, have minimal impact on your blood sugar level at all, and cannot be seen as good sources of energy (though perhaps valuable for vitamin/mineral or fibre content).

The index is a comparative one, using glucose as its reference. Glucose, being a pure simple sugar, is metabolised very rapidly. It is given the value of 100. All the other foods which have been tested are compared to that value. Therefore, a food with a glycaemic index of 100 would be available for use by the body just as quickly as glucose, whereas one with an index of 50 would take twice as long to achieve the same level. Carbohydrates with an index of 50 are excellent sources of fuel for the runner. Lower than that, they probably do not provide adequate fuel, and higher than that, they will probably be depleted too quickly. You may be surprised, as you look at the selected list of common foods and their glycaemic index, to see that many foods which are starches, and traditionally thought of as 'fuel' are actually quite high on the index, and not that well suited to your running requirements.

How much carbohydrate is enough?

If you want the exact specifications, you'll be glad to know that you need five to ten grams of carbohydrate per kilogram (2.2lb) of body weight, depending on the amount of exercise. This means that approximately 60–70% of your diet should be carbohydrate based. It is a daunting task to figure out grams per kilogram when you are not a trained nutritionist, so don't go that far, unless you want to. Here are a few ways that you can tell if you are fuelling yourself correctly.

Baked potato	98
Rice bubbles	95
Carrots	92
Honey	87
Pumpkin	75
Weetbix	75
Watermelon	72
White bread	69
Raisins	64
Bananas	62
Sweet corn	59
Kiwifruit	58
Rice	52–72
Yam	51
Spaghetti	50
Sweet potato	48
Shortbread biscuits	48
Baked beans	40
Apples	39
Lentils	29
Cherries	23

Figure 22: Glycaemic index of some foods

– Do you feel 'well-fuelled'? A lack of energy can come from many sources, but weight loss, accompanied by hypoglycaemic episodes, as described here, might be an indication of inadequate carbohydrate intake.

– Do your meals centre around a carbohydrate dish? The traditional fare might revolve around a piece of meat, with a few vegetables on the side. If, on the other hand, your main meals include a rice or pasta dish, you are headed in the right direction. In order to achieve the high carbohydrate intake that I describe, you will have to avoid fat, and high fat foods.

If in doubt, you can start by keeping a three-to-five day record of all that you eat and drink. With the help of some nutritional guidebooks, it may be clear to you that you are, or are not, consuming 60–70% of your intake in the form of carbohydrates. If you are still in doubt, consult a professional dietician, and preferably one who has experience working with athletes and active, healthy adults.

Changing dietary habits to include adequate carbohydrates

You can also make some adjustments that would set you up for adequate carbohydrate intake. If each of your main meals is centered, as suggested above, around a carbohydrate-based dish, you will be starting off on the right foot. The following suggested menus show modifications which can be helpful for bringing enough fuel

---

HYPOGLYCAEMIA
– A runner's nightmare!

It is a beautiful Saturday afternoon, and you plan a lovely run. You got up later than usual and had a light breakfast. The kids didn't head off to school and your routine is different. You lingered over coffee and nibbled a piece of coffee cake. And what with getting the kids off to their sport, doing some grocery shopping and hoeing the garden, you threw together a light lunch. Quick! Get in a run before everyone gets home. You go out for about an hour.

After a few miles, you have a gnawing feeling of hunger. 'Should have eaten more!' You start thinking about chocolate but keep running, but it doesn't feel quite as nice as usual. You feel weak, almost wobbly, and that's frustrating. You wonder if taking three days off was a good idea after all. Maybe you're not as fit as you thought. You start to feel worse. You're a bit sweaty, and your fingers, toes, and lips are a bit tingly. You start craving, big time! You sight honeysuckle flowers climbing a wall and practically eat the vines, remembering how nice the nectar tasted as a kid. You're running as slow as a walk but it feels just as hard as a marathon. You finally make it home and throw yourself on the fridge, wolfing down everything in sight. Immediately refreshed, you realise that you had simply run out of fuel!

Meal	Traditional	Carb adapted
Breakfast	Fried eggs & bacon Toast and butter Coffee and full milk	Porridge & raisins Yoghurt Orange juice Coffee with low fat milk
Morning Snack	Danish pastry Coffee and full milk	Apple Water crackers and cottage cheese Tea with low fat milk
Lunch	Egg salad sandwich Coleslaw Oatmeal biscuit	Filled roll with lettuce, grated carrot, cucumber, tomato and cottage cheese Oatmeal biscuit Apple
Afternoon Snack	Peanuts Chocolate milk shake	Popcorn Apple juice
Dinner	Pork chops Spinach Mashed potatoes (with butter and milk) Apple crumble	Stir-fried pork on rice Spinach/tomato salad with vinaigrette Banana Biscuits
total protein: **total fat:** **total carbohydrate:**	**15%** **53%** **32%**	**14%** **24%** **62%**

Figure 23: Comparison between traditional and carbohydrate-adapted meals

into your diet. These are purposely quite traditional types of meals, to show how it can be done in the most ordinary of circumstances. Ethnic variations are usually not a problem, as rice, grains, pasta and breads are the high-carb base of culinary habits all over the world. Vegetarianism, as well, provided it is well planned, adapts beautifully to a high-carbohydrate diet.

When to fill up?

Another consideration to take into account when concerned with energy intake for running is when to eat. You may have noticed that if you run right after a meal, you don't feel well. You may be rewarded with 'the runs' (diarrhoea), or with general feelings of malaise. If you don't eat at all, you don't feel much better! What is the best way to fit in the feed?

If you run too soon after a meal, you may be bothered by 1) a stomach which has not had time to empty properly, and by 2) blood sugar disorders. It would seem that with a meal fresh in your body, the supply of sugar in your blood would be excellent, but in fact, in some individuals, elevation of the blood sugar which follows a meal causes the hormone insulin to come around and hasten the removal of the excess sugar from circulation and put it into storage. That means that after an initial rise in blood sugar, there can be a subsequent fall due to this increased storage feature, which will cut down on your ability to provide fuel to your muscles. Hence, the need for some people to avoid running directly after eating.

The same phenomenon can occur when you eat foods which have a high glycaemic index all by themselves. If you eat 'high index' foods, but accompany them with other foods which are metabolised more slowly, they will relay to keep your blood sugar high enough for exercise. The sugar high provided by high-index foods alone creates insulin secretion. (An example of this would be eating jam without bread). To avoid the other extreme, that of running on empty, it is desirable to eat foods which are placed in the mid-range of the index, one to three hours before exercising. This means that if you have breakfast at 7:30am, but plan to run at noon, a mid-day snack is important. I find that after-work runs are often very difficult if I haven't snacked. If you lunch at 1:30pm, and run at 6:30pm, you'll find once again that the fuel reserves are low.

One additional thing to keep in mind is that snacks can easily end up being high in fat. Fats slow the digestive process by delaying stomach emptying. That is why they are so satisfying. They make you feel 'full'. That delayed stomach emptying can be a problem for a runner, as it can lead to gastric upset. Try to avoid

---

HIGH-CARB SNACKS

granola bar

bagel and honey

dry fruit and biscuits

popcorn

wholemeal bread and jam

blueberry muffin

english muffin and marmalade

porridge and raisins

fruit juice and biscuits

---

snacks that are high in fats (crisps, peanuts, commercial pastries), salt or heavy seasoning.

After running, more carbs!

Another important time to focus on carbohydrate intake is after the run. When you go for a particularly long, or hard run, you deplete your muscle supply of glycogen (remember, glycogen is the form in which carbohydrates are stored in the muscles). Researchers have discovered that the best way to restore your glycogen reserves after intense exercise is to consume a generous amount of carbohydrates as soon as possible after exercise.

When you come in after a hard run, that is the perfect time to have a nice glass of fruit juice, and a few pieces of bread. If you do not have a full meal within the next two hours following exercise, it is recommended that you repeat that high carb snack a second time. These recommendations are mainly related to hard runs, or quality work-outs, when you come back fatigued from your exercise. Too much food, be it carbohydrate, fat *or* protein, will be stored in your body as fat.

Carbohydrate supplements

You can buy sports drinks and sports bars which are designed to contain high levels of carbohydrate. This can be attractive in many situations. If you don't have time to get together a good snack, and nothing is available for purchase at work, a sports bar with adequate carbohydrate content may be just the thing to sneak into your back pack, or hand bag. If you have a fast metabolism, and find that you are regularly running out of fuel during the working day, or on the run, a high carbohydrate drink or bar may be just the thing you need to help you out. There has been a recent proliferation of brands of sports nutritional supplements. Which is best for you? Check the label or request information from the manufacturers. American publications, such as *Runner's World* and *Running Times* often contain special articles on nutritional supplements. Please check the bibliography for other references.

PROTEIN – nutritional building blocks

Protein is essential for muscle and body growth, and for the repair of damaged or injured tissues. An active exercising woman needs to ingest 1 to 1.5 grams of protein per kilo of body weight (2.2lb), which is close to 12–15% of total dietary intake.

High quality protein is readily available in flesh foods, such as meat, poultry and fish. There are however,

Suggestions for dishes with adequate protein/carb balance for distance runners

Chilli beans (vege) and rice with grated Edam
Green salad + oil and vinegar
Banana
• protein 24% • fat 27% • carb 60%

Chilli beans con carne with rice
Coleslaw + yoghurt dressing
2 pancakes with lemon juice and sugar
• protein 15% • fat 28% • carb 57%

Stir fried chicken with vegetables on vermicelli
Banana
Ice cream
• protein 23% • fat 22% • carb 56%

Macaroni with tomato sauce and cheddar
Lettuce and cucumber salad + oil and vinegar
Apple
• protein 12% • fat 44% • carb 43%

Tofu and vegetable sauce on rice with sesame seed topping
Steamed broccoli
Corn on the cob
Yoghurt
• protein 17% • fat 22% • carb 61%

Chicken and chilli stuffed baked potato
Garden salad + oil and vinegar dressing
Apple
• protein 17% • fat 22% • carb 61%

Food	Protein
Parmesan cheese	40
Soy beans (dried)	35
Swiss cheese (gruyere)	29
Wheat germ	29
Tuna	25
Chick peas	24
Chicken	21
Beef	18–20
Other fish	18
Pork	16
Eggs	13
Oysters	10
Bread	8
Peas	6
Milk	3.5
Rice	2–4
Cheddar cheese	25
Tofu (firm)	16
Tofu (medium)	10

Adapted from *Equilibre alimentaire et sports d'endurance*, by Denis Riché, Vigot Press, Paris

Figure 24: Protein content of common foods (per 100 grams)

non-flesh, and non-animal sources for protein as well. Figure 24 highlights some of the common protein sources, and their relative protein content.

Increased physical activity requires a similar increase in protein intake, of 20 to 30%. Protein is used up more quickly in older exercising adults, so for runners over the age of 40, a careful look at adequate protein intake is important. Remember, as mentioned above, a salad diet won't cut it for a committed runner who is putting in regular training.

FAT
– a dirty word?

Fat has a wicked reputation in the health field, and yet we all need some food sources of fat. Fat is a high energy source, supplying almost two times as many calories as protein or carbohydrates. Furthermore, some vitamins which are important to health can only be brought into the body through fat-containing nutrients (liposoluble vitamins). A no-fat diet would not satisfy your body's needs while exercising, or any time for that matter!

So why are we so hard on fats? Probably because most people in developed nations eat more than they need, and the consequence of that is heart disease, obesity, and increased risk of certain cancers. Why do we eat too much fat? Mainly because fats are hidden in so many of the foods we eat. No one would think of sitting down and eating butter or oil by the spoonful, but meats, cheeses, sauces, condiments and cooking techniques all bring additional fats to our daily ration. Running women need to understand how fats can affect their running, so as to use them judiciously.

Fat is used as an energy source, as we discussed above. It is mainly used for low intensity exercise. This doesn't

Food item	% Fat	Alternative	% Fat
Fried chicken with skin	15.7	Grilled skinless chicken	7.3
Coleslaw (traditional)	5.5	Coleslaw with lemon juice dressing	0.0
Madeira cake	16.9	Crusty bread rolls	2.3
		Bagel, pita pocket	1.4
Pork chops	27.4	Beef cube steak	7.4
		Steamed cod fillet, grilled tofu	4.8
Potato chips	33.4	Popcorn (hot air popper)	2.0
Cheddar cheese	35.2	Edam cheese	26.0
Tuna salad (mayonnaise)	33.0	Tuna salad (yoghurt)	18.0
Bagel and cream cheese	10.0	Bagel and hummus	2.0

Figure 25: Alternatives to high fat food items

mean that we should eat fat in large quantities in order to 'tank up', however, because all excess nutrients (including carbohydrates and protein) are transformed to fat in the body anyway. It is best to restrict the amount of fats to 25% of the total diet. This seems to be well below the level at which they have negative effects on overall health.

Fatty foods are often savoury and appetising. They take more time to be digested, so they give a better sense of 'fullness', or of having satisfied your appetite. They can take upwards of five hours to get out of the digestive tract! This can be a disadvantage to a runner. If you have any digestive sensitivity, and you have had a high fat meal prior to running, you may find that you are very uncomfortable while on your run. If you have digestive problems, you may want to take a closer look at what you are eating to see if the 'hidden' fats in your diet are actually too high.

There are ways you can adapt your cooking styles to accommodate a lower fat intake, without sacrificing taste. Instead of frying, or saute-ing, try steaming vegetables, and grilling meats and fish. You can then **season** with fat, instead of cooking with it. A teaspoon of olive oil or melted butter would be inadequate to fry potatoes, but would still impart the butter taste. Low fat cook books are readily available, and

may be of some help. Don't substitute 'no-fat' for 'low-fat', though, or you will be in a bad way.

OTHER DIETARY CONSIDERATIONS

Water

You need more water when you run than you do in regular situations. Water makes up a very large part of your body, and is vital in order for many of the metabolic actions to take place. Without adequate hydration, energy stores can not be used properly, dissolved minerals can not be put to their intended use, nor can you maintain the blood pressure required for good performance.

As a runner, your water needs increase for several reasons. The elevated muscle activity of running produces excess heat which is regulated, among other ways, by the secretion of perspiration. The amount of perspiration varies from one individual to another, and depends on weather conditions as well. You also lose water through breathing, as witnessed by the cloud of vapour that you can see each time you exhale on a cold day. As your respiratory rate rises greatly with running, so does your water loss. The increase in muscle activity requires more water. A healthier lifestyle may also result in your having more frequent bowel movements, which once again uses significant amounts of water.

It is thus quite important to ensure adequate fluid intake. It is likely that at least two litres per day, and probably more, will be necessary. The best way to determine if you are drinking enough is by the amount you urinate. You should urinate frequently during the day (six times at least), and your urine should be clear and not concentrated. Water is the drink of choice, but juices and other drinks can be substituted. Do not use caffeinated drinks as a source of hydration, because the caffeine has a diuretic effect which makes you more likely to be dehydrated.

The legendary 'eight glasses a day' are probably an underestimation of the fluid requirements of a runner. Three litres would be much closer to adequate. Water may seem particularly bland and hard to drink. Or, it may have a chlorinated, or metallic taste. Here are a few hints which can help you take in enough water.

If the water doesn't taste good:
- The colder the water, the less you will taste it. Keep a big jug of water in the refrigerator at all times.
- Add a few drops of lemon juice, or a sprig of mint to mask the flavour. Keep away from syrups, and sugary mixtures, however.

- Buy a small water purifier to attach to the tap for drinking water.

If you just don't like drinking:
- Try drinking from a sport drink bottle, or from a straw. Sucking may be more your style, than sipping. (Don't laugh! I was a non-water-drinker for years, until I realised how much more I liked drinking from a straw. I have no trouble putting away three litres a day now!)

Some women will retain fluid during certain times of the month (usually when pre-menstrual). Water retention is not a reason for restricting fluid intake in normal circumstances.

Calcium

Calcium is important in making strong teeth and bones. Adequate calcium intake is an important investment in long-term bone strength, and in the prevention of osteoporosis in later years of life. Weight-bearing exercise, such as running, also helps contribute to strong, dense bones. Female runners need more calcium than sedentary women. The recommended daily requirement of calcium is 800–1000mg in adult women. It is thought that women runners probably need closer to 1200mg, and this outside of pregnancy, or breast feeding, at which time requirements are higher still!

With inadequate calcium intake, future bone strength is compromised, and the risk of stress fractures increases.

In order to achieve the level of 1200mg of calcium per day, you will need to drink five glasses of milk (full, low fat or skim, it doesn't matter), or five servings of Edam or Gruyère cheese. Caviar, incidentally, is high in calcium, as are watercress, almonds and cider. It may be that your eating habits do not include enough calcium-rich foods. If this is the case, and if it seems unlikely that you will be able to eat (or drink) the quantities described, it is certainly appropriate to speak to a registered dietician about dietary supplementation. Calcium supplementation is safe and relatively inexpensive, and may constitute the best choice for you.

Iron

Many runners, and especially women, have been found to have iron deficiencies. This can be due to inadequate iron in the diet, heavy menstrual blood loss, iron loss through sweat, and red blood cell destruction from the pounding of feet on the pavement. A low iron level can affect performance and your health. It is important to maintain adequate iron intake.

The best dietary sources of iron include lean red meat, liver and kidney, poultry and fish, but also some non-flesh

foods including pulses such as kidney beans, or baked beans, and whole grain cereals. It is also important to consume enough vitamin C, as it enhances iron absorption. Taking iron supplements is not the best way to get adequate iron. Unlike calcium, taking iron can have negative effects. Risks include digestive discomfort, decreased absorption of other minerals, and even heart disease and cancer. So, don't supplement needlessly. Only take iron if it is prescribed by your physician after a blood test.

Caffeine

Caffeine is a stimulant. You may have heard that it is thought to enhance performance, and many marathon runners believe that strong coffee before a race will help them to run their best. It may be that caffeine delays the onset of fatigue in distance runners. This benefit is hotly debated. Coffee is not without undesirable side effects which can negatively affect running, and well-being in general, so using it as a possible (though controversial) performance enhancement agent is not advisable.

Caffeine is also a diuretic. This means that it increases urine output, and as a result, decreases hydration. Therefore, coffee is not a good fluid replacement source, as it actually decreases the fluid available for use. If you have spent the morning drinking coffee, you will not have had the benefit of the fluid volume you have drunk, as you probably have urinated more than you have taken in due to this diuretic effect. Furthermore, coffee may create gastrointestinal disorders, such as diarrhoea or sour stomach, which will also have a negative effect on your running.

We all know about the stimulating effect of coffee. It raises your heart rate,

and may increase your blood pressure. If you are taking oral contraceptives (birth control pills), or are in the latter stages of pregnancy, caffeine is cleared from your body two times more slowly, so the effect may be increased, and prolonged.

Does this mean we should quit drinking coffee and caffeine-containing drinks altogether? No, it does not. You should just recognise the effects that caffeine has on your system, and tailor your intake to your own reaction. You should not consume caffeine with the specific intent of improving your performance, because it is not clear that the effect is positive; because the International Olympic Committee has included it on its list of banned substances; and because there can be negative (even dangerous) side effects from taking too much caffeine at once.[14] On the other hand, don't stop drinking coffee or caffeine-containing substances cold-turkey. Caffeine does have a mild addictive effect, and if you withdraw in an abrupt manner, you will probably find that you have headaches, and feel very sluggish.

---

14 For more information on the consequences of the use of caffeine as a performance enhancing substance, please consult the excellent book *Drugs and the Athlete* by Gary I. Wadler and Brian Hainline, F.A. Davis Company, Philadelphia, 1989.

Pre-race nourishment

Many of the books referred to in the bibliography will provide you with information about pre-race dietary preparation. The only advice I would like to add is that a dietary modification will only work if it is suited to your personal needs. You must discover what works best for you and use it. Don't make any major dietary changes the week or the night before a race. Introduce changes gradually, and adapt them to fit your lifestyle. The best recommendation is that a well-balanced, high carbohydrate/low-fat diet will get you through most races. Specifically tailoring a diet to an event, although often quite helpful, is not always necessary.

Over-eating

We eat for many reasons. Nourishing our body is one of them. Others include pleasure, boredom, routine, depression, rebellion...the list goes on. If you are like me, and like most people, you do not necessarily wait to be hungry to eat. I find that working night shift makes me eat indiscriminately. I immediately launch into a bag of crisps as soon as I get to work, even though I am not hungry, and don't usually eat crisps. And likewise, as soon as I wake up the following afternoon, I am immediately drawn to the kitchen. 'What can I eat?' I think, despite having no feelings of hunger. Food seems to help me to cope with my disturbed sleep/work patterns.

The fact is that we have been brought up to see food as being more than it is. We were often congratulated on eating, and punished if we didn't finish our plate. As a result, it becomes difficult to separate food from the emotional role it was given us as children. If we punish ourselves for eating outside of hunger, we are much more likely to continue to use food for reasons other than nourishment. On the other hand, if you are, like me, an over-eater, it is probably a good idea to pay attention to your motivational forces when you eat for non-hunger reasons. Am I hungry? No, I am not. I am bored. Is there something else that would make me less bored besides food? No, not right now. Okay, eat! And enjoy it!

This recognition of the reasons for your feeds may actually help you to reduce the non-hunger eating sessions. Advice on overcoming the over-eating problem can be found in the book *Overcoming Overeating – Living Free in a World of Food* by Jane R. Hirschmann and Carl H. Munter, Addison-Welsey Publishing Company Inc.

RUNNING AND BODY IMAGE

When you look in the mirror, what do you see? Do you ever get surprised by your reflection in a shop window when you are walking downtown, and think, 'Do I really look like that?' Do you see yourself as a stranger, or as someone you know quite well? Do you like what you see? Do you hate the way the top of your thighs jiggle, or how pale your face seems, or that awful slouch that you wish you were disciplined enough to correct? Why are we so hard on ourselves? Why are there so few women who are happy with the way they look?

Women often have distorted images of what they look like. Despite objective measures like skin fold measurements of body fat, height and weight which show a well-balanced weight, many women persist in wanting to reduce their weight further. They are often attempting to achieve unrealistic and illogical goals which do not match their morphological types.

The 'perfect' woman, as suggested by the media and by current fashion design, is a tall and very slender waif-like individual: an unachievable standard for most of us. As a result, many women fill themselves with the guilt of not achieving what they perceive as the desirable standard. According to therapists Jane Hirschmann and Carol Munter, 'Eighty per cent of adult women feel they are too fat and want to

15 *Overcoming Overeating – Living Free in a World of Food*, Hirschmann and Munter, Addison-Wesley Publishing Company, Inc., 1986, p41.

make themselves thin. Why thin? The male of our species is, by nature, thinner, harder, and more muscular than the female, who is rounded and curved by fat deposits on breasts and hips. Why does a woman strive to be more like a man? Because despite the great inroads women have made, men continue to have more power and control.'[15]

I can remember watching a world championship triathlon out of the corner of my eye, while doing something else. I was thus not listening to the commentary. The first woman zoomed by on her bike. I can remember thinking right away, 'She's a big girl. Look at how powerful her thighs are!' ('Powerful' is a

code word for 'big' in the waif-speak.) The camera then focused in on the next two participants. They were both wearing high cut briefs and racer back tops. They had exceedingly long slender legs, with excellent muscle definition. 'Wow!' I thought to myself, 'what legs!' – secretly wondering if my own legs might compare favourably to such specimens. Well, the announcer came on and identified the mystery legs. They belonged to the first and second place male competitors!

Would it not seem pathologically silly to want to look like men? Hard legs, heavy muscle definition, straight hips...we deny our gender! Here's Hirschmann and Munter again: 'Change Your Shape and Change Your Life is about power and control. All of us who play are attempting to recreate ourselves, to become someone we are not.'

Casting a strict judgement on our bodies affects our entire life. Self-worth is influenced by our personal perception of our selves. When we judge our bodies severely, we also end up questioning our entire self worth.

Runners are regularly confronted with their bodies and their body image. Changing clothes and revealing parts of the body which are usually covered by everyday wear exposes us to the view of others, and to their (and our own) judgement. Being a runner implies a kind of self-control and mastery. Not being as slim as you want may make you feel that you have let yourself down. Often a runner may feel over-weight because of being unaccustomed to exposing so much flesh, and particularly, so much leg. But there's no need to wear skimpy clothing if you don't feel comfortable with it. Sweat shirts, pants, leggings and track suits are all available in a wide range of fabrics, sizes and designs.

Studies have shown that women who exercise do have more positive feelings about their bodies than sedentary women. That's great, but keep distinguishing between your health, and your weight. Weight is not the best measure of fitness. You should be feeling strong and energised and have a good appetite.

Many runners enjoy the fact that running helps them to keep weight off. In a society where thinness is seen as a symbol of success, that aspect of running is indeed attractive. Running becomes a way of controlling your weight, and possibly your life. Unfortunately, eating disorders are not uncommon among women athletes. In an attempt to control their weight and their lives, women with eating disorders may run excessively, while following a rigid and inadequate diet.

Out of the thousands of women who run every day, all over the world, all body types will be represented. Tall and short, slender and plump, runners of every imaginable size will be found. Sometimes, the fastest runners are remarkably stout. A woman's weight, and even less, the size of her thighs, doesn't measure fitness. Even a very corpulent woman may in fact have a low percentage of body fat, while an apparently skinny woman may be in an unhealthy range of body fat percentage. So you can't just look at someone (or at yourself) and think, 'Oh, they should lose weight!' any more than you can step on the scale and know that you are overweight.

If you want a particular 'look', you should probably keep that in mind when you are choosing your parents. Okay, so no one asked your opinion when you were conceived. That means you have to take the genetics the way they were dished out. Likewise, you can't go back in time and tell your parents that a high fat diet in childhood will set you up for a given number of fatty cells that you will not be able to rid yourself of. You can reduce the volume of those fatty cells, and change the way you look overall, depending on development of muscle groups, but you can't make them disappear. At puberty, hormones will grace you with fat deposits that you did not have previously: at the top of your thighs, in your lower back, on your hips. Some women will have more than others, but no pill, cream or massage gadget will make it all evaporate. Even running won't

work miracles. It may make fat deposits less apparent, but that is all.

You need some fat

There is a good reason to have some fat on your body. Without fat, we would not have enough insulation. We would be cold, and susceptible to illness. Fat is a good source of energy for low intensity activity. You do need to have a reasonable amount of fat.

To know if you have too much or not enough fat, you can't just step on the scale, or look in the mirror. The scale can't take into consideration your build, the weight of your bones or muscles. Your own eyes won't be objective enough. You want to find out what your percentage of body fat is. An approximate determination of your body fat percentage can be made by a variety of different techniques. The golden standard is underwater weighing. This technique is cumbersome, and available in only very limited settings. Essentially, in underwater weighing, a determination of lean body mass is made by weighing an individual on a swing while submerged in water. This weight, when compared with normal body weight, will show body fat percentage.

Such precision is not necessary in non-research settings. More commonly, the measurement of skin folds is used to determine body fat percentage. Special callipers are used to measure skin folds in areas of the body that are considered representative of total body fat. The sum of the skin folds can be used to predict the body fat percentage. There is a margin of error in this technique but it is much more accurate than the kind of weight predictions you might find in fashion magazines, on weight charts or from well-meaning friends. If you wish to know your body fat percentage, or are concerned about whether your current weight is reasonable, discuss this with your doctor. He or she will be able to advise you.

Once I know my body fat percentage, should I try to change it?

Body fat percentage is only one indication of overall condition. If you are eating properly, and exercising regularly, your body fat percentage should reflect that by being in a healthy range. It is probably more important to pay attention to your diet and your exercise than it is to worry about your body fat percentage.

Are you eating three balanced meals a day? Are your snacks nourishing and necessary? Do you treat yourself to a yummy food binge only every now and then? Are your meals prepared without excessive hidden fats? Do you drink enough fluids? If you can answer these questions affirmatively, you are off to a good start. Are you exercising regularly (at least three times a week, every week)? Do you get enough sleep? Do you avoid consuming excessive alcohol?[16] With more 'yes' answers to these questions, you are certainly on the right track. Your weight, your figure, and your body fat percentage are likely to be in the proper range for your body type.

If, despite following the proper food/exercise regimen, you still feel heavy and ill at ease, seek professional assistance. As I stated at the beginning of the book, there is no magic recipe, and I can't possibly advise everyone across the board without seeing, talking to, and knowing them. This is an example of a case where you should contact your doctor or dietician for advice. It is important to feel comfortable with the person you consult. If you are not, find someone else!

Losing too much weight is obviously not desirable. Even elite athletes, who are exceedingly fit, can get caught up in the trap of seeing their weight, or their body fat, as being a predictor of form, rather than looking at their real well-being and performance levels. If your body fat drops too low, you'll become sensitive

---

16 Alcohol contains plenty of calories. There are about 7 calories in 1 ml of alcohol. This means that a glass of wine or beer contains around 100 calories.

to cold, and easy prey to infections. Running will be hard because you'll be more easily fatigued. You'll be more susceptible to injuries, and to menstrual irregularities, with all that entails (see chapter five). It is much more important to focus on the more relevant predictors of form and well-being than it is to centre your concerns on weight and body fat.

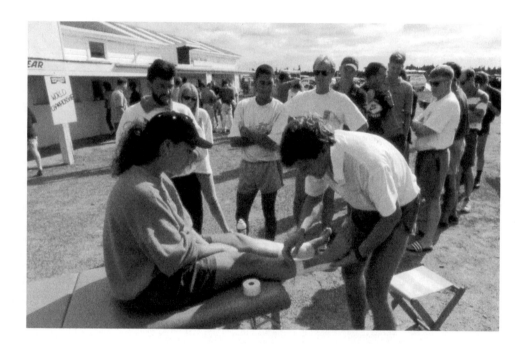

CHAPTER SEVEN

Running Injuries and their Prevention

Running has so much to offer. On the other hand when we get unreasonable, or excessive, we can actually do ourselves harm through running. It is funny to think about injury in a non-contact sport. It seems so safe! It is one of the safest sports around, as long as we use common sense while we are practising. On the other hand, running is not a panacea which will suddenly make us more practical, or more sensible. As a result, most runners will get injured at some point in their running. Please read this chapter prior to having any injuries. The preventative measures are quite easy to take, and they will save a lot of heartache down the road.

The injuries incurred while running are not usually related to trauma. Occasionally, a runner might twist an ankle, stumble off a track, or, heaven forbid, be involved in a motor vehicle accident. The main cause of injury in runners however, is repetitive movement and impact. When you go for a 45 minute run, you may take as many as 9000 strides. Any biomechanical quirk with which you were born will be emphasised 9000 times, with greater force than when you walk.

IS THIS AN INJURY?

Maybe one day while going for your regular run, you feel an unusual pinch or jab in your calf (or foot, or knee...). It may not even stop you from running, but you notice it. It is different from the usual stiffness you might associate with running, but it goes away, so you don't pay it much mind. Maybe, the next day, you feel the jab (pinch, ache...) in exactly the same place, but it doesn't go away so quickly. It stays there for the entire run, and you can still feel it when you get home. It may or may not bother you in your activities of daily living.

Hopefully, at this point, you say to

yourself 'Oops! Old body's trying to tell me something!' and you take a few days off, or go swimming or biking instead, and things come back to normal. If you are like most of us, you may instead say to yourself, 'Oh, what a pain! I bet it's just a freak thing. What's more, I have been planning all week on taking a long run on Saturday with Tom, Dick and Harry, and I wouldn't give that up for anything. I don't usually get such good company for my runs! And then there is the 10km next week. I certainly don't want to get out of shape, just because of some tingle in my leg which is probably nothing anyway.'

In your advanced stage of denial, you may indeed persist in your training, ignoring the message, and whoops! On Saturday, the leg is rather worse than better, you have to stop running because you are starting to limp, and the following days, it hurts enough that you are not able to run at all, and you have to give up the idea of the 10km race altogether. You are injured. If only you had listened to your body!

So that is how running injuries usually appear: discreetly and inconveniently. Once you realise this, it will be very helpful in the prevention of future injuries.

Another fact to recognise which can help you to ward off injury is that you don't lose all the fitness you have acquired when you take off a few days, or even a week or two. It makes a lot more sense to sacrifice a few days to fend off the niggle, than it does to lose several weeks or more, to a fully established injury. Although running remains the most convenient form of exercise for most of us, we can find replacement activities when we must. Swimming, biking, rowing (or rowing machines in a gym) are all excellent cardio-vascular exercise and may not strain the affected area. You can 'run' in the water if you are not a swimmer. With a wet vest, or simply a flotation device of any kind strapped onto your back, you can go through the movements of running, without the impact factor. This may or may not work for you, depending on the type of injury.

The first thing I do when my legs or feet start hurting is to look at my shoes. They may look pretty good, but how long has it been since I had a new pair? According to some researchers,[17] running shoes retain, on average, only 75% of their initial absorption value after only 50 miles of running. After 100 miles, the value is down to 67%, and from 250–500 miles, the shoes only absorb 60% of their initial absorption capacity.

With this thought in mind, it is pretty clear that if you have worn your shoes for a while, the soles will be quite packed,

---

17 Cook, D. S., Kester M. A., Bruret, M. E. *Shock Absorbing Characteristics of Running Shoes*, The American Journal of Sports Medicine 13, 4, 1985.

and you may suffer from the reduction in shock protection. This may be the cause for your discomfort. As an elite runner, I have usually had the good fortune to have my shoes supplied by a sponsor. This means that I am able to change my shoes as I see fit, without concern for the expense, and certainly every 1000 miles. If you are on a tight budget, keep your eyes peeled for good sale prices, and stock up on your favourite models when possible. That way, you are not compelled to suddenly buy new shoes at a time which is financially difficult.

If, on the other hand, you have just purchased a new pair of shoes, and your problems coincide with the change in footwear, it may be that the new pair are not well suited to your needs. Have they actually exaggerated a foot strike or biomechanical problem that had not bothered you in the past? Put your old shoes back on, and see if things improve. If so, get new shoes, but the same as the old model. Stick to what works! In many cases, all it will take is finding a pair of shoes which are better suited to your needs than those you were wearing at the onset of symptoms. Examine the sole. Is the new shoe curve lasted,[18] while the other was straight (or vice versa)? Is there more (or less) flexibility to the sole? Is the new one significantly lighter (or heavier) than the old? Look carefully at wear patterns of the soles and the uppers. Reread the section on the choice of shoes, and discuss your new shoes with an experienced running shoe dealer.

R.I.C.E.

After taking care of the running shoe issue, when my legs are niggling I apply the R.I.C.E. treatment. R.I.C.E. is an acronym for Rest, Ice, Compression and Elevation. That means, put your legs up, ice the sore spot, wrap it if appropriate, and take some time off running.

It is pretty straightforward, and will take care of many problems. It will not remove the cause of the injury, but it will treat the result, and calm down the inflammation while you are examining what is wrong. I will usually consult one of the books I have on running injuries,[19] not so much to self-diagnose (not very trustworthy), but to get an idea of what kinds of injuries may cause the discomfort I am feeling. Once I know that, I may be able to modify my activity to avoid any aggravation. There are some common running injuries which can be identified, such as Achilles tendonitis, or shin splints, with some standard treatment recommendations. This is helpful to know.

If R.I.C.E. and a change of shoes have made no difference, it is time to seek out

---

18 See shoes, Chapter 1.

19 See 'Recommended Reading'.

a physician's advice. Here, it is most important to consult someone with experience in athletic injuries. As a health care professional I hate to admit that it takes a truly exceptional physician to understand and treat athletic injuries properly if that is not an area in which they specialise. Keep this in mind. Your GP may indeed be one of those special doctors. If not, find out who takes care of the runners in your town, or consult a doctor who runs him/herself. Follow the treatment and advice you are given, and hopefully, everything will sort itself out.

HOW TO KEEP INJURIES FROM OCCURRING

- Keep yourself in well-adapted, new(ish) shoes. We have discussed why.
- Run on a variety of surfaces and courses. Don't run solely on the footpath, where the impact is brutal. Similarly, don't run exclusively on soft tracks, beaches or grass. These surfaces require a great deal of adaptation and stabilisation. Although the initial impact forces are less, the reaction forces are greater. Don't run only on the hills, or only on the flat. If you can vary your training sites sufficiently, you will reduce the repetitive stresses which may cause injury.

- Don't over-extend yourself. If you increase your mileage too quickly, or if you don't give yourself adequate rest after a period of increased training, your body will not have time to reinforce itself, or consolidate, and you will break down. Plan regular rest as part of your training, and take it! Get enough sleep, and don't burn the candle at both ends. Your lifestyle must allow sufficient recovery. If you are having trouble sleeping, cut back your running. If you stop menstruating, take it very seriously. Follow the advice in chapter five.

- Use your training diary effectively. The training diary is a very helpful tool for tracking leg soreness, early onset and history of injury, and can be helpful in the diagnosis, management and prevention of the injury. Noting shoe changes in your diary can be of further assistance in the monitoring of causes of injury.

- Make sure your diet is adequate. Is your calcium intake high enough? Are you eating enough protein? Are you taking in enough fluids?
- Are you a compulsive stretcher? Do you use stretching to replace a natural warm-up period of gentle running which is important before digging into a hard run, or speed work-out?

When your body complains, it is usually because you have exceeded your own personal limit. You can't shrug it off because the nagging injury won't go away simply because you will it so. What one person can do, another may not be able to. Injuries come as a reminder of your own tolerance, your personal limits. When you become injured, treat yourself properly, and look at means for reducing unnecessary stressors in your life.

Injuries can be stressful in themselves. If running is a coping mechanism, or a stress management tool for you, you will find yourself very ill-prepared to deal with this unplanned glitch. You may become angry, or depressed. You may find yourself thinking about your injury, and imagining the worst possible outcomes. The injury may become an important focus in your daily life, as your running usually is. Concentrating on injury is certainly not the best way to regain health. Instead, refocus your attention on productive alternatives to running. If you can't run, find replacement exercises. If you can't exercise, read all those books you had always promised yourself you would. Knit a sweater (furious knitting is an excellent stress release!) or make a model plane. Renew old friendships. Write letters. There is always something to do, and you will have excess energy while you are waiting for your body to recover.

A WORD ON STRETCHING

Stretching is often heralded as the magic anti-injury prevention tactic. Some runners will refuse to go out the door before they have performed their

---

A few cardinal truths about running injuries

1. Getting injured is a sign that the body has failed to adapt to the activity that you are doing.
2. Serious thought and analysis must be given to the injury in order to treat, cure or prevent.
3. The greatest risk in running injuries is re-occurrence within 12 months, so run oh-so-carefully during a post-injury period.
4. Never accept as a final opinion the advice of a non-runner (Tim Noakes, *The Lore of Running*).

---

pre-run stretching routine.

There is little medical literature on record to directly address the place of stretching in an injury prevention programme. One very large study reviewing the prevalence of injuries in a group of 1680 runners over a twelve month period[20] was interested in which factors were most likely to lead to injury. Failure to stretch was not a risk factor, but the research findings suggested that runners who use stretching 'sometimes' are at apparently higher risk than those who usually or *never* use it. These researchers found that high mileage was the only consistent cause of increased injury.

This finding was later confirmed by another survey study of 1505 athletes.[21] Another 583 runners were studied by researchers from the University of South Carolina, to look, once again, at what factors might be responsible for injury in long distance runners.[22] They concluded that the risk factors for injury were high weekly mileage, a history of running related injury in the previous twelve months, and inexperience.

It would be wrong to be lulled into a false sense of security, that because you stretch you will be less prone to injury, or that when you have signs of impending injury, you can 'stretch it away'. On the other hand, a proper warm-up prior to undertaking any athletic exercise is advisable, if only to prepare the body for the change in activity level.

20 Walter, S. D., Hart, L. E., McIntosh, J. M., Sutton, J. R., The Ontario Cohort Study of Running Related Injuries, *Archives of Internal Medicine*, November 1989, Vol. 149, pp2561–2564.

21 Brunet, M. E., Cook, S. D., Brinker, M. R., Dickinson, J. A., A Survey of running injuries in 1505 competitive and recreational runners, *The Journal of Sports Medicine and Physical Fitness*, Vol 30 (3), pp 307–315.

22 Macera, C. A., Pate, R. P., Powell, K. E., Jackson, K. L., Kendrick, J. S., Craven, T. E., Predicting Lower-Extremity Injuries Among Habitual Runners, *Archives of Internal Medicine*, November 1989, Vol. 149, pp 2565–2568.

Conclusion

It is difficult to finish this book. It is noon, and as is my habit, I turn off the computer, change clothes, and go out for a 56 minute run with my lunchtime running group. Chances are, if today is like most days, over the course of those 56 minutes, or in the post-run cogitation, I'll come up with yet again, another personal discovery of some brilliant gift that my running has offered me. It is an endless exploration. Every day, every stride, makes me more aware of the depth of discovery yet remaining, and brings me closer to a better understanding of my self and of my world.

The adventure that I live through running has given me everything of value in my life. It has given me self-esteem and confidence, through the discovery and understanding of my body. It has opened up horizons and introduced me to the people who have become my mentors, my friends and my family. It seems silly when I think about it lucidly, that putting on a pair of shorts and trotting around the neighbourhood, would contribute to my well-being in such a stupendous way. Well, it may just be that in order to make the most of my life, I have to first make the most of my physical fitness.

As a health care professional, I am aware how important being involved in our own health can be. We can either get on the train of life, and just take a ride, or we can actually go up front, and give the driver a hand! Active participation in your own health, fitness and well-being is perhaps the most enriching thing you will ever do.

Happy Running!

Appendix

RECOMMENDED READING

Gloria Averbach, *The Woman Runner, Free to be the Complete Athlete*, Cornerstone Library, 1984

Anita Bean, *The Complete Guide to Sports Nutrition: How to Eat for Maximum Performance*, 3rd ed, A & C Black, London, 2000

Allen Guttman, *Women's Sports – A History*, Columbia University Press, New York, 1991: Women in sport, from ancient Egypt to the twentieth century.

Karen Inge and Christine Roberts, *Food for Sport Cookbook*, Simon & Schuster, 1989: A comprehensive guide to designing a nutritional programme for athletes of all ability levels.

Fred Lebow and Gloria Averbach, *New York Road Runners' Club Complete Book of Running*, Random House.

Timothy Noakes, *The Lore of Running*, Oxford Press, 1992: Simply the most valuable reference book about running ever written! Historical analysis of training techniques, in-depth discussion of physiology and injuries, meticulous cross-referencing.

Mona Shanghold and Gabe Mirkin, *The Complete Sports Medicine Book for Women*, Fireside Books, New York, 1988: Written by distinguished researchers in the field of women's fitness, with a special interest in gynaecological and obstetrical concerns.

The Runner's Literary Companion, edited by Garth Battista, Breakaway Books, New York, 1994: Great stories and poems about running.

Joan Ullyot, *Running Free, A Guide for Women Runners and their Friends*, Perigree

Books, 1980: Essentially the first useful book on women's running by a physician, pioneer and inspiring runner.

Grete Waitz and Gloria Averbach, *World Class: A champion runner reveals what makes her run, with advice and inspiration for all athletes*, Warner Books, New York, 1986: A valuable book written by the 'grande dame' of the women's marathon. Includes inspiration and training tips.

Kathrine Switzer, *Running and Walking for Women over 40: The Road to Sanity and Vanity*, St Martin's Press, New York, 1998.

USEFUL NAMES AND ADDRESSES

UK Athletics
Athletics House
10 Harborne Rd, Edgbaston
Birmingham BI5 3AA
ww.ukathletics.org

London Marathon Ltd
PO Box 1234
London SE1 8R2
www.london-marathon.co.uk

London School of Sports Massage
(with nationwide directory)
28 Station Parade
Willesden Green
London NW2 4NX
www.massage-therapy.demon.co.uk

Running Fitness
Emap Active
Apex House
Oundle Road
Peterborough PE2 9NP
www.on running.com/runningfitness

Runner's World
7–10 Chandos Street
London W1M 0AD
www.runnersworld.co.uk

Organisation of Chartered
Physiotherapists in Private Practice
Cedar House, Bell Plantation
Watling Street
Towcester
Northants NNI2 6HN
www.physiofirst.org.uk

WEBSITES OF INTEREST

www.womens-running.com

www.avoncompany.com/women/avonrunning/

www.runnersweb.com/running/rw_womens.html

Index